Tapping the Source

Deanna ~
Tap On
always

with love .
Barbara Catalano

Tapping the Source

Tap Dance Stories, Theory and Practice

BRENDA BUFALINO

A WOODPECKER BOOK

CODHILL PRESS

New Paltz, New York

Copyright©2004 Brenda Bufalino

Published by Codhill Press, Inc.
1 Arden Lane
New Paltz, NY 12561

Book design by Will Marsh

Library of Congress Cataloging-in-Publication Data

Bufalino, Brenda.
    "Tapping the source" : tap dance stories, theory and practice / by Brenda Bufalino.
    p. cm.
    ISBN 1-930337-15-9 (alk. paper)
    1. Bufalino, Brenda. 2. Dancers–United States–Biography. 3. Tap dancing. I. Title.

GV1785.B833A3 2004
792.8'092–dc22
[B]
                                                                2004056116

10   9   8   7   6   5   4   3   2   1

Printed in the United States of America

Contents

For Jeb and Zach
and to my students,
who inspire me and help me to know who I am.

ACKNOWLEDGMENTS

Thanks to Sandy Burlingame, who supported this effort with her encouragement and generous time spent editing. And thanks to Susan Hebach, Tony Waag, and Barbara Duffy for reading the manuscript and suggesting important inclusions.

~

Introduction

BEYOND THE STORIES of the tap renaissance from the 1970s to 2000 and beyond. Beyond the study of composition and choreography, the revelation of tap techniques explored and developed by Honi Coles and myself, *Tapping The Source* examines how the environment can shape an artist: how the environment is the landing pad from which the artist spreads his or her wings and takes off . . . then closes the wings and lands to regroup in familiar territory.

If there is an architecture to the creation of dance, does a dancer (me) believe, feel, and instinctively understand that a dance, like a Frank Lloyd Wright building, should be part of its environment, like an extension of a rock cropping hanging over a cliff? Or does the dancer (not me) see his or her creation as like a Corbusier building, existing in space and unrelated to its elements? My work grows out of nature, like a leaf from the tree, like lichen on a stone. I have always believed that impressions are an artist's food. The taste, look, and feel of what's around me, what I see or identify and take into my body, heart, and mind, mix in my unique blender to make the cake I dance upon.

More than anything, earth, wind, water, fire, and creatures are the inspiration for my dances. The motivator is

the wind, which pushes my body into the studio to practice. The instructor is the insistent squirrel whirling its
dervish dance, hiding its treasure, finding its treasure
. . . the chickadee braving a winter song, singing sunlight
into the snow, melting the ice with its melody . . . the deer
stealthy and watchful, surveying the grass under a stand of
pines before bedding down on its needles.

And while I look deep in my heart for its genetic map, I
also search the sky for unknown constellations. I feel the
myriad of influences, tastes, and textures of my mixed-
blood background and rejoice with the voice that chooses
to tap through me, only to be replaced or joined by
another voice tomorrow. I am filled with gratitude for the
many voices that sing through me. I dance and write my
monologues as a tribute to my many influences and
impressions. They are refrains that live in all my brothers
and sisters of the world, yet they blend in me in a unique
way. These influences condemn me, enslave me with their
insistent call, but also embrace and liberate me with possibilities to create something unique, a new clear voice not
copying any of the known melodies.

My body, its shape and contours, strengths and weak-
nesses, also determined what I have created. I started out
lean and mean, in right proportion for a ballet dancer, but
with flat feet and a fiery independent temperament. At
eleven I morphed into a voluptuousness that took me by
surprise, more like a panther than a Giselle, with big
breasts and buttocks, calves and thighs, pulling me into the
earth as well as lifting me through the air.

As a jazz, Afro-Cuban, and calypso dancer I responded
to the call of gravity, the drumbeat of the throbbing earth.
There was no choice in that, simply an inevitability that I, a

girl from New England of mixed parentage – Scotch, English, Native American, Italian – would dance my way into jazz, into native and indigenous cultures, to find the tools and techniques for my creations. It was inevitable that I found myself at fifteen dancing beside black and white bodies who agreed that dance was like praying, giving back to the earth an answer to its call – and my response was tapping rhythms and howls of songs. Was I denying my European heritage when I was fourteen? That's what my first modern primitive and jazz tap teacher, Stanley Brown, suggested when he told me to go home, that I would never be happy in an environment of African rhythms, forms, and shapes. But that was my home as much as any home and any place was home.

Stanley was wrong. In spite of my struggles with gender and race, I find it is happiness to claim all of yourself, to be the sister to all the sisters in the world, and in yourself. Answering all the calls that insist on being answered and shaping a technique out of them creates a dance of inclusion. A multitude of rhythms blend gently, fiercely, sometimes in combat, sometimes in a soft embrace, sometimes lustfully conceiving a new planet of sound and movement. Listen . . . and you might hear how the planet sings, how the earth, sea, and sky insist their rhythms into our hearts, and how we respond and co-create when we are tapping the source.

BRENDA BUFALINO

"SINGIN' SWINGIN' & WINGIN'"

"Every step
she executes
has its own
intricate joys."

--BACKSTAGE
Joel Garrick

The Ballroom

253 West 28th Street between 7th & 8th Avenues

New York, New York 10001 • 212-244-3005

With the
Amy Duncan Trio

Wed-Sat at 11pm

Part one

A Tapper's Life

ONE

~

Early Training

Home Schooling

IN 1937 I WAS PREPARING FOR MY DEBUT into life under the layers of organdy that camouflaged my mother's swelling belly. She was seventeen and had the starring role in the Gilbert and Sullivan operetta *Iolanthe* in the seaside town of Swampscott, Massachusetts. She said that I was very active and my rhythmic kicks in her womb insisted themselves upon her arias like a drumbeat.

Like many little girls who grew up during the era of Hollywood musicals, I was sent to dancing school at the age of five. When I wasn't in dancing school, I sewed costumes for my dolls or sang "I'd Like to Get You on a Slow Boat to China," standing under the streetlight on top of the hill in front of my grandparents' house at 50 Banks Terrace in Swampscott. My family didn't find my evening recitals for the neighborhood embarrassing because they were all musical and would dance or sing anytime, anywhere, for anybody. Nana Lena had a rich baritone voice and played the piano. Grandpa Strickland played the fiddle. Aunt Gloria, a coloratura soprano, practiced day and

15

Family picture: Alfred, Brenda, (age 3 or 4), and Marjorie Bufalino.

night on the big grand piano that overwhelmed Nana's tiny living room.

My mother, Marjorie, a lyric soprano and an elocutionist (dramatic reader), brought me to tears reciting "Has Anyone Seen My Mouse?" from the A. A. Milne stories of Christopher Robin.

Every Sunday, after the big New England boiled dinner of corned beef and cabbage or clam chowder with homemade biscuits and molasses, the whole family gathered in the parlor for our musicale. Everyone was expected to participate, except for my father, Al Bufalino, whose talent was ballroom dancing, and my baby brother, Tom, who was yet to show any signs of musicality. Under the rug separating this modest living room from the dining room, a three-by-four-foot maple floor produced a beautiful high-pitched tone when my taps shuffled to the vocal accompaniment of "Strolling Through The Park One Day," "On The Bumpity Road to Love," "Somewhere Over the Rainbow," or

"Lovely Hula Hands." Though I only knew a few steps and didn't know a *shuffle* from a *cramp roll*, I danced to every tune my aunt and mother sang, turning at the end of a *time step* and interjecting some pantomime or acrobatics; my hyperactive energy created the illusion of lightening speed.

In 1943 I was six years old. My father was in the Air Force, and Mom worked at the fruit stand. Alone most of the day and much of the evening, if I wasn't at my grandparent's house I occupied myself doing solo pirouettes and cartwheels in my back yard, spinning to keep dark and dangerous spirits from ascending into my unprotected and empty house.

Professor O'Brien's Normal School of Dancing

If I wanted to go to dancing school I had to get there on my own. My pilgrimage began at the old yellow train station across from our house on Burrill Street. I traveled daily on the Boston & Maine Railroad to Professor O'Brien's Normal School of Dancing in Central Square, Lynn. It was a frightening journey most of the time. In the winter Central Square was dark when I arrived. The sidewalk outside the small taxi office was illuminated by a single yellow light shining dimly through a smut-stained window. A few round-bottomed patrons sat on the stainless steel stools of the doughnut shop eating jelly doughnuts and drinking cup after cup of Maxwell House coffee. Ghostlike shadows stood in line waiting for their bus or just leaned against doorjambs waiting for nothing.

For five years, six days a week, I climbed the two flights of stairs over the Essex Trust Bank to Professor's school. How extraordinary to find, in this small, abandoned shoe town, such a brilliant and eclectic teacher of dance – ballet, Egyptian, interpretive, Spanish, acrobatic, and my favorite, tap dance.

The early training for a tap dancer, like that of a ballet dancer, is of paramount importance. As a young dancer I learned basic tap vernacular and such excellent technique that I would not have to correct my action later.

Professor O'Brien taught me my first manipulations of *flaps, shuffles, riffs, cramp rolls, wings,* and *pull-backs,* and my first steps – s*huffle off to Buffalo, falling off the log, Maxi Fords, trenches,* and the basic *time step with a break.* He taught beginners so clearly and emphatically that we never had to relearn these basic manipulations or steps. I established very few bad habits, except for rubbernecking and sticking out my tongue when I concentrated, often biting the tip when coming down out of a *wing.* Professor taught tap dance with the same specificity that he taught ballet, and he felt that all dancers should learn tap dance before ballet for rhythm training and musicality.

Mrs. O'Brien, who always dressed in black with her gray hair tied sternly in a bun, accompanied all of her husband's classes on the piano. Her range of musicality was wide and vast, from the waltzes of Chopin to Ravel's *Shéherazade* and Fats Waller's "Ain't Misbehavin'." She played flamenco music, Arabic music, and tunes from Tin Pan Alley. Her repertoire was endless.

Professor dressed in the same kind of khaki pants every day and a white shirt. His hair was white and his skin was very white. He gave commands with his arms crossed while his older students demonstrated. The piano vibrated against the quiet of the room as we circled in our white tunics, our arms taking the shape of ancient Egyptian hieroglyphs. The dance was suffused with spirit and mystery. Early in my training I learned that dance could change how I felt inside, rearrange my moods from sad to happy, angry to content. Dance altered my emotional and physical behavior from anxious hyperactivity to purposeful action. The confines of my world expanded. After a day trying to navigate a young life of lonely trials and confusion, dance class helped me focus my body and gather my wandering thoughts into a single point of attention. Expressing my emotional life through music and movement convinced me that art had a purpose; it electrified the air and gave the six o'clock hour more sparkle than any other hour of the day.

Professor didn't believe in recitals. He felt his job was to teach students the discipline and philosophy of dance, not to dress them up in frilly costumes to gratify their parents or set a swollen ego upon a fragile young soul. What he did in lieu of a recital was to invite our parents to watch a class every three months. After our dance demonstration, still dressed in the same class costume, the white tunic with colored sashes, we stood at attention behind Professor looking like a band of angels while he lectured our parents on the careless way we were being brought up. The lecture I liked best was the talk on lying. He suggested to our parents that their children would never learn to tell the truth because of the bad example they, as parents, were setting. "You lie constantly," he said, "with big lies and small, but worst of all you lie to yourselves."

Our parents sat with their hands folded during his scolding. They accepted his stern lectures because he charged only three dollars for six days of classes, and everyone had a relative who had learned to dance from him. When my grandfather was a boy he taught ballroom for

Professor, and in later years they were brothers in the order of Masons, both achieving third degree. Professor had as much to do with building my character as developing my body and spirit. I knew from the start that I would have to observe and correct my wayward behavior if I wanted to stand tall and measure up to his standards when I grew up.

Though I didn't have the opportunity to dance in a yearly recital, after a few years of study I was on the road with my mother and aunt, performing club dates and concerts at Rotary Clubs and lodges of the Eastern Star and the Masons. Our act was called the Strickland Sisters.

Because of the rushed, always late, hysterical atmosphere of these road trips with my grandmother, mother, and Aunt Gloria, I developed a distaste for performance. My costumes were never finished, my shoelaces always came untied, and the floor was always too slippery. Tears backstage followed the smiles that fooled the audience. If some mysterious and passionate inner spirit had not insistently driven my body to dance, I might have ended my career at a very early age under the severe gaze of a wooden Indian facing the stage of the Swampscott Elks Club.

Alice Duffy's School of Dance

In 1948, when I was eleven, my route changed after a confrontational episode with the Professor. I challenged his dictatorial rules and became more interested in my appearance and in the impression my dance made on an audience. I began to travel on the bus through the circuitous winding streets of Salem, past the Witch House and historic mansions topped with widows' walks, to Alice Duffy's School of Dance. Miss Duffy introduced me to theatricality,

Brenda Bufalino in Hawaiian skirt her father made from parachute strings that became costume for Hawaiian dance routine.

props, and gimmicks. She created dances for our class with jump ropes, top hats, canes, and suitcases. She created solos for me on roller skates and pedestals. All of these dances were crowd pleasers, but she never sacrificed clear articulation for flash; we were both clear and flashy.

We had an accompanist who created musical arrangements for every dance. Miss Duffy, in her blue one-piece jumpsuit and Bette Davis bob, clacked her castanets anytime the rhythm was off. There was no margin for error when it came to keeping time.

In contrast to Professor O'Brien's philosophy of art without artifice, Miss Duffy began preparing for recital the first class of the year. We paid for our spring costumes when we registered in the fall.

When I was fourteen, my mother, who was singing ballads and swing tunes in nightclubs around New England, brought her booking agent, Sam Drake, to my last Alice Duffy recital. After seeing me dance in leopard-skin tights with a bright magenta bustle and a hat with horns to a jazzed-up version of Ravel's *Bolero,* Sam thought that I would excel under Stanley Brown's tutelage in Boston.

Stanley Brown's Studio

In 1950, the day after my fifteenth birthday, the Boston & Maine Railroad took me to Stanley's studio on Massachusetts Avenue. This was the defining moment of my life as an artist, and I knew it even before I entered his studio on the second floor over the movie theater. Dressed in a pink dress, white pumps, and white gloves, I was covered with sweat as I breathlessly climbed the stairs. Uninvolved, as in a dream, I was simply following the destiny and a course that fate had long ago set out for me.

I discovered real jazz when Sandy Sandiford or Dean Earl accompanied our classes, playing hot swing on the upright piano. The little girl from the white sands and blue-green ocean of Swampscott felt newborn and charged with electricity when dancing Afro-Cuban to the poly-rhythmic throbbing of three drummers crowded into the corner of Stanley's studio.

Stanley Brown was a proud West Indian man who opened his Boston studio after a very successful career in vaudeville. He was associated with many of the great black dancers and entertainers from the movies, nightclubs, and musical theater. They came to the studio often to dance and to teach. Professional artists would also perform with us in our recitals, which were presented with all the pro-duction values of a Broadway musical. Original arrange-ments were created for each number, accompanied by a rhythm section and at least two horns.

Stanley was my first rhythm tap teacher. I worked with him privately. He would show a phrase and then leave the room, expecting me to perfect and execute it using my own intelligence, style, and intuition. The first tap solo that he created for me was to the tune "How About You?" I thought it was the corniest, squarest, silliest song I had ever heard. I cried when I met with our arranger, Sandy Sandi-ford, "I hate this song." With the cigar stuck between his teeth he mumbled, "Don't worry, sweetheart, you're going to love it when I get through with it." Because of his trans-formation of a tune I thought was so corny into an arrangement so swinging it almost danced the dance for me, I learned that *It's not always how the tune is written that makes it great. It's how you play it.*

With this realization in my pocket I began a lifelong study of arrangements created for the Count Basie, Duke Ellington, and Cab Calloway bands, as well as those created for Frank Sinatra, Mel Torme, Ella Fizgerald, and other vocalists that I loved.

At sixteen years old I was a physically well-developed professional performing in nightclubs with "The Bobby Clark Dancers." Underage and with a phony ID, I knew it was dangerous to be dancing in an interracial review in the very conservative city of Boston, performing African rituals and French cancans. Of course, I also had my tap solo to "How About You?" and danced African contractions in bright red toe shoes for our version of "The Red Shoes." I also used that phony ID to sneak into jazz clubs every night after a class or a performance to listen to the New Orleans jazz of Doc Cheatam, the modern jazz of Maynard Ferguson, and the bebop improvising of young saxophone players. Throughout the next two years I shaped my style through the music that I loved.

By my seventeenth birthday I felt the confines of the Boston show business circuit that many variety artists called the "graveyard." It was said by the acts that played clubs in Revere, Lawrence, and Lowell that there was always plenty of work, but you could never get enough money to get out of town. I was ready to try my luck and further my studies in New York City. Stanley suggested I look up Charles "Honi" Coles and Pete Nugent in their new studio, Dance Craft, on 52nd Street.

New York City was the last place my parents wanted me to go. My father was very old-fashioned and had already said goodbye when I left home for Boston. Now he figured that I was on my own to live with the consequences of my decisions. My mother was very busy, as usual, with her own career and had long since given up holding me hostage to a life of comfort and security. They wished me well over the phone, and once again I took the train, alone, to unknown places. I found a very short-lived and unfortunate living situation in a condemned building on the Bowery — a building with crumbling staircases and no running water but plenty of running cockroaches. After an exhaustive search I finally took an apartment over Jilly's Black Magic Room on 52nd Street, just a block away from almost everything I needed in music, dance, or theater. In 1955 it was still possible to walk down Broadway with your portfolio filled with photos and reviews, walk into one of the many agents' offices, and get a gig for the weekend that paid at least forty dollars. The nightclubs, theaters, and Broadway shows were no longer booking tap dancers, and a few shots on the Ed Sullivan show were about all a hoofer could hope for. Honi Coles, known as a class act with the fastest feet in the business, couldn't find a floor to dance on, so he opened a studio called Dance Craft with Pete Nugent, another out-of-work class act who was part of the famous trio Pete Peaches and Duke.

First Apprenticeship with Honi Coles

Soon after I arrived in New York I became a protégé of Honi Coles, a tap dancer who played his feet like a jazz musician. He was so fast and his arms and legs so stylish that he took my breath away. He started out with a *time step,* but he never seemed to return to it. His ideas stretched out into long phrases, or he would take a simple step like a *cross step* and add taps, turns, and slides to it, dressing up this plain old step in jewels and satins until it hardly resembled its humble origin. He sang his steps and he sang tunes as he danced. He didn't need any music; he was a one-man band. His manipulations were varied and exciting, both visually and rhythmically. His feet took on a personality. You could almost see them smile.

After winning amateur shows with his flashy tap Charleston, Honi had begun his professional career dancing on pedestals with the Miller Brothers. He then joined up with two other tall handsome dancers to tour as the Lucky Seven Trio. Finally, he and Cholly Atkins got together after the Second World War and created the celebrated act of Coles and Atkins, performing with big bands and on Broadway in *Gentlemen Prefer Blondes*. He had a lot more difficulty booking his solo act. So dense and complicated were his rhythms that agents told him to come back when he had a routine.

Swing was his element, but his tap licks anticipated the bebop era with their run-on phrases not necessarily closing at the end of a bar. Even though his own phrasing was unconventional and modern, he didn't like to dance with bebop drummers like Art Blakey who laid "bombs" all over the place, drowning out his taps. He much preferred Joe Jones, the maestro of swing, who kept fabulous time with the stylish delicacy of his brushes. Joe Jones, a tap dancer himself, knew how to leave space for the dancer.

When I studied with Honi, it was more like a collaboration than a class. Rhythm tap dancers basically felt you could either do this form or you couldn't. You were a swinger or you weren't. Nobody could teach you to swing. Picking up a phrase from Honi Coles in the 1950s was an extremely creative act. He never used the words *shuffle* or *flap*; he found them nonsensical. He transferred his information by scatting either with the feet or with the voice. *Shuffle-ball-change a flap brush step step* would be translated to *shubededo badupadobop.* Honi had a pet saying that remains true to this day: *"If you can sing it you can do it. If you can't sing it you can't do it."*

I wasn't the only girl dancer in those waning tap years at Dance Craft. Pete Nugent's protégé was a beautiful, long-legged, talented blonde with the appropriate first name of Eve. Watching them dance was like watching angels descend from heaven. Pete traveled and utilized the whole floor. Even though many of his figures looked familiar, derived from Eddie Rector's dance named after the tune "Bambolina," his elegant execution and delicate delivery were from a world I had never known. The live acts I had worked with, even if they were from a jazz background, always pushed to sell. I had never seen class acts like Pete Peaches and Duke or Coles and Atkins in performance, nor was I familiar with their subtle delivery of a step. I soon understood: *It's not always the step itself but how you execute it that makes it ordinary or incredible. A simple figure, executed with style, wit, and clear articulation, can become even more effective than flashy turns or complicated trick steps.*

The dancers at Dance Craft expanded my rhythm and performance perceptions and inspired my desire to develop my own tap dance voice even as the venues and audiences were disappearing.

Training in the World of Calypso and Jazz

Though most students were no longer including tap in their repertoire, other forms were thriving. New York City in the fifties was wall-to-wall dance. I took jazz classes from Matt Mattox and Bob Hamilton, and Afro-Cuban and modern-primitive from Sevilla Forte, Talley Beatty,

Walter Nix, and Chino. I studied all day, every day, and performed at night when I could get a gig. I hardly displayed caution, descending through underground tunnels and subways or deserted late-night streets, trudging from one jazz club to another. I listened and absorbed. After my gigs performing Afro-Cuban or calypso in Brooklyn or Long Island, at four in the morning it was up to Harlem to hear an after-hours jam at the 125 Club. When I wasn't working I'd go to Small's Paradise, Birdland, Basin Street, Jimmy Ryan's, or dance the mambo at the Palladium with Machito, Tito Puente, or Joe Cuba's bands. These clubs were my universities. I felt ushered into the kingdom of the musical gods when I performed in an Afro-Cuban trio choreographed by Chino at the Palladium on Wednesday nights, and on the *Spanish Hour* every Sunday night on channel thirteen, in front of the same Latin bands I idolized.

I didn't have a lot of company when it came to listening to the modern jazz of Charles Mingus or Max Roach and Clifford Brown. The older tappers I knew still preferred to dance and listen to Basie, Duke, Cab, or Lionel Hampton.

By the time I began studying with Honi, tap was already on its way out as a popular performance dance. Though he considered himself an impresario of sorts and wanted to help me navigate my career, to his disappointment it was always my Afro-Cuban or calypso act that got the work. Tap dance was relegated to the Monday night jam sessions with out-of-work dancers at Dance Craft. At these sessions dancers accompanied themselves by humming, singing, or playing stop-time chords on the piano.

This was the climax of my tap education — improvising, and trading four and eight bars with some of the greatest dancers I had ever seen or heard. With no tap students to support it, Dance Craft closed in 1957. There were no more Monday night jam sessions, and Honi Coles, tired of looking for jobs when there weren't any, went to work as stage manager for the Apollo Theater in Harlem. Tap dancers took work wherever they could find it, and most hung up their shoes, never expecting tap to come back.

My studio training ended when I was nineteen years old, but the gifted words of my brilliant teachers were firmly secured in my unconscious where I could retrieve them when stymied, lost, or in despair. It was time to teach myself what could not be learned from someone else.

The greatest difference between the tap training of today and of yesterday is in the relationship to the music. In all my young years of study and performance I never had the occasion to dance to taped music or records. Unlike students today, who have never had the good fortune of being accompanied by live music, I never had to wonder where a bar began or ended on a CD. My relationship to music has been as intimate as the sound of my own taps.

Two

~

The Avant-Garde & Free Jazz

BY 1960 EVEN THE VENUES where I found work singing and dancing "Back to Back and Belly to Belly" or playing my conga drum while singing "Calypso Blues" were closing. The Calypso Room, the African Room, and Café Society in New York and the Blue Angel in Chicago had kept me working four shows a night seven nights a week for two years. Suddenly not only had tap dance disappeared, rhythm itself began to seem out-of-date.

Confused and exhausted I retired for a while, married and gave birth to a baby boy. I wrote plays and poetry. I stopped dancing, but I didn't stop listening to music.

Jazz was being played free and out of time. Improvisations were no longer related to a bar structure, and indeterminate collective improvisations were built more around abstract ideas than linear notes dancing up and down a music chart. I couldn't imagine a place where I might fit in.

In 1962, between changing diapers and watching *Diver Dan* on TV with my two year old, I switched the channel and heard some very modern and free music accompanying a painting exhibition on the CBS program *Look Up & Live*.

This Sunday morning, religious-arts program featured many contemporary artists and emerging musical forms. To my surprise the music that so engaged me was composed and played by my old friend from Boston, Ed Summerlin. The music inspired my poetry and made me want to dance again. My old friend was on to something, and I wanted to become a part of it.

When we began music and dance collaborations, Ed told me quite frankly, "Forget about the rhythm because we have moved on to free music. We've got to eliminate the boundaries and create new forms . . . make theater with our music . . . mix up the mediums . . . synthesize." He told me to listen to Ornett Coleman, Steve Lacy, and Stockhausen, composers and players who were really saying something new.

Motivated by the same desire to leave the confines of New York City for the country, Ed's family and mine found abandoned buildings in upstate Dutchess County. His family moved into a schoolhouse in Clinton Corners, and my husband and I, with our growing family which now included a second baby boy, began renovations on a very old church in LaGrangeville.

Finally our ideas found space in which to develop. Our imagination was spurred on by the hardships of trudging through the snow to backyard outhouses and climbing steep inclines to fix leaky roofs and broken windowpanes. While I was returning to the land and dancing amongst the pines, I was creatively entering the concert world of the avant-garde, free jazz, and happenings.

After putting my sons to sleep I sat late at night on the altar, where prayers had once evoked spiritual passions, and wrote poetry. Ed gathered this poetry and composed music to my rhyming rhythmic musings. He was composing for the National Council of Churches at the time, perhaps the most supportive venue for art, jazz, and avant-garde music in the country. In the 1960s many of the more liberal Protestant sects were exploring ways to enliven their liturgies and create services that were intellectually challenging, celebratory, and confrontational. Roger Ortmeyer, the head of the Arts Council for the National Council, brought some of the country's most innovative artists to both parishioners and general audiences. Painters, musicians, actors, and dancers were exploring the relevance of faith and hope for salvation in a nuclear world amidst the cold war with Russia and the hot guerilla war in Vietnam. The work was often abrasive in response to the world around us. We felt stranded and abandoned in a country which was polarized, rich against poor, and old against young.

My poems were not created as lyrics, and I was always surprised at the collaborative outcome. What a thrill it was when a collective of outstanding musicians – Bob Nordin on trombone, Ed Summerlin and Don Heckman on saxophones and clarinets, Charlie Mariano on drums, Ron Carter on bass, and vocalist Sheila Jordan – performed my poem "Of a Sudden I Saw a Star" in a tiny church in Millbrook, New York.

> *I went round the corner*
> *climbed upon a bus*
> *Up the hill firefly bar lights passed*
> *I left behind the crawling snakes of streets*
> > *And heats of hate*
> *Salvation Army hostages*
> > *A broken shadow leans against its bricks*

The cats fight between the fat ladies' legs
And leap upon the flowing garbage heaps
The girl flees from her lover
Into the arms of another
To hover
Gang boys corner teeth a glitter
Gleaming piercing eyes into the gutter
I pass another store
Another sausage hanging . . . forevermore

Sudden darkness, there are no streets
　　Night lights heat
Great God there's sky and of a sudden I saw a star

Soon after that debut, in the summer of 1966, Ed was cooking up something big for a Methodist church in Pine Plains, a little hamlet just a few miles from his school-house. It was to be a whole weekend of happenings, beginning with a play called *The Hairy Woman* performed, by the Hamm & Clove Theater from New York City. Ed chose my poem "The Living Ash" for a new composition. Rosie Unutmas sang and I danced with intermittent vocal recitations while projections of liquid colored oils swirled overhead. The last stanza of the tune was actually written in 4/4 time. Ed allowed just a few measures for my lyrics and dance to swing.

　　. . . Last dawn the sun sighed
　　Last day the lambs cried
　　Last night everything died
　　And all the wolves returned
　　The flowers smothered by the ferns

And all the books were burned
   Eyes polished
   Children washed
   Time abolished
   Mother emptied all the trash
   Looking for the crimson ash
   That I may know
That someone ever lived at all

The event was sublime chaos. Toward the middle of the
service, we performed Don Heckman's musical composition *Convention*. My part was to read *Sex and the Single Girl*
through a bullhorn and occasionally improvise a set of cal-
isthenics while the band played a cacophonous blend of
Sousa-like marches and old war songs in two or three different keys. I was as uncomfortable as I had ever been in a
performance. I couldn't figure out what this cacophony had
to do with jazz or the liturgy. Finally, in the middle of the
piece, I was unable to continue and sat down in the front
pew. I needed to listen. As I absorbed the raucous com-
mentary on our way of life and the hoopla and farce of the
political convention along with the tragedy of so many
boys dying in the Vietnam War, I began to understand
what we were about. I returned to the pulpit to dedicate
myself to the process of unfolding mayhem for the rest of
the weekend and the next ten years.

It was a great exploration. We traveled from town to
town and state to state across the Northeast, performing in
sanctuaries where unwary parishioners were definitely
awakened from any complacency or peaceful morning nap
they had hoped to sustain through their Sunday service. I
wrote text for both concerts in theaters and celebrations in

small or grand churches, but all music and presentation was improvised on the spot.

I would lug props, which gave me inspiration and a focus inside these free improvs. If I picked a license plate out of my performance suitcase, it inspired an idea, as did a length of rope, cardboard boxes, flashlights, masks, toys, and noisemakers.

This chaotic creative period freed my spirit; I could dance again without the slavish pandering to a half-drunk audience in nightclubs. I could pay attention to the making of art, and the audience had to find its way to the path that led to the door of meaning. It also introduced me to the idea that I didn't always have to dance in tempo. I could dance jazz rubato, dance around the time, break the time apart, and return to it. My dance was more interpretive. And I could be a part of the music, work within an ensemble but still maintain my own voice. I was part of the band.

In the 1970s Ed was composing and I was dancing to his new synthesizer creations. Of course, I couldn't tap dance, since everything we did had to be a new idea, and the art world as well as grant organizations were enthralled with technology. Yet I carried my tap shoes everywhere, just in case.

In 1973 I finally had the chance to integrate my past with my future. Ed and I were booked for Charlotte Mormon's Avant-Garde Festival at the South Street Seaport in New York City on a boat, the *Alexander Hamilton*. Our position on the boat was the bottom, in a cage, wired in like animals. Ed placed his synthesizer in the center of the cage, and beside him I placed a barrel for me to dance in and out of. I tied a rope around my waist and began to climb around the wire cage like a monkey, occasionally lowering

myself into the barrel for a rest. Ed accompanied my tra-
peze act with electronic reverbs and screeches.

The whole boat was electronic. Video installations of
Nam June Paik were stacked from floor to ceiling. Everyone was wired and dressed in silver Mylar fabric — one
hundred wired and weird artists with the expectation of
performing without stopping for twelve hours. On the
twelfth hour Charlotte Mormon, in a diving suit, would
descend into a water tank with her cello and a tape
recorder. It wasn't long before Con Edison's gift of electricity would short circuit from the overload. All performances
came to a halt.

I had my tap shoes in my suitcase. Ed had his saxophone. I took off the rope, untangled myself from the wire
of the cage, and put on my shoes. We started to jam, actually working four to a bar, just tap dance and jazz in an
Avant-Garde Festival. It felt like heresy — outrageous, confrontational. The patrons on the boat, with nothing electronic to view and listen to, surrounded our cage ten deep.
We were an acoustic sensation. No one had heard or seen
tap dance in fifteen years. "What a trip! Far out," everyone
exclaimed.

As I continued to introduce tap to the avant-garde by
putting my rhythms through the synthesizer that Ed
manipulated, it all began to feel familiar. Just what was the
difference between an avant-garde performance and a
vaudeville show I wondered. Is there a way to blend the
presentational performance of a variety entertainer with
the introspective and expansive concepts of a concert artist? That moment and that question presented me with the
two stools I have sat and danced upon throughout my

career. As a tap dancer, am I an entertainer or an artist? Is tap dance music or is it dance?

Throughout my career I have attempted to blend many diverse theatrical, musical, and choreographic elements into one presentational canvas. My successes or failures often result from the way these elements come up against each other, how the segues or edges soften before a contrasting structure is introduced.

Life seems to be like that. We don't live on one plane at a time. I leave my solo existence in the woods under the pines and head for a performance in front of two thousand people, two contrasting themes. But in between there's a car ride and a plane ride — a segue. And there is the structure for a new dance.

THREE

~

The Tap Revival
& Great Feats of Feet

IN 1973 I SEPARATED FROM MY HUSBAND after fourteen years. In all those years of remodeling old houses and the church in LaGrangeville, as well as building an organic farm from scratch, I never had my own dance space. There is nothing like having your own studio to work in, to take your time, dream, and experiment with actualizing visions, big and small. I was indeed very fortunate when my friends Karl and Ann Rodman discovered an old abandoned carriage house that had also been used as a car repair shop. After buying the building, Ann renovated this decrepit space; downstairs she created a craft shop for herself called Handmade, and upstairs, for me, a beautiful, barn-wood studio with an oak floor and mirrors, which I named The Dancing Theatre.

We occupied our new businesses in 1974. She began her store with ladders and hay bales for surfaces, and inside the lobby, under The Dancing Theatre sign I hung a poem: *A small offering / is all a sparrows song / tilts lopsided on the air.* This was a reminder that I needn't feel trapped or frightened by the confines of a business—to remind me that this was a space in which to create. It would be a temple of dance, not a factory. Here I taught a blend of Afro-Cuban, modern jazz, avant-garde, and eventually tap.

At The Dancing Theatre I presented other artists in performance and new works in a friendly informal atmosphere. I performed my one-person show, "At the Junction." This was a multimedia piece with poetry, song, mixed-genre dance and tap, accompanied by Andy Wasserman on piano, sitar, and conga drum. As I continued to perform this piece and incorporated more tap dance into every show, the encores and enthusiastic reception for

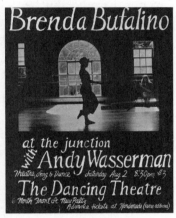

my percussive improvisations made me feel that the audience was eager for its return. I decided to give my full attention to tap dance.

At that time, specializing in this form seemed an unlikely, even foolhardy choice because there was no place to perform tap dance and no one to dance with. So I began to teach at SUNY New Paltz in the continuing education department. When planning the course description the curator asked if there was not some way to make the class title, "Tap Dance," sound hipper. I suggested, and they accepted, "Hoofing," a pejorative term signifying that the dancer danced close to the floor and didn't move around much. Yet, those of us who like to think we can play a concerto on a three-foot-square piece of wood consider being called a "hoofer" a compliment. The class was taught in the Old Main Building on campus, which had a perfect, crisp, maple floor. It was only used for rock concerts, and nobody every bothered to clean up the empty beer bottles, candy wrappers, or crushed soda cans after a big bash. While the dance students lined up against the torn black curtains, I would shuffle through the garbage to get to the stage and put on the single overhead work light. To my surprise students filled every class I offered, and as I discovered ways of teaching this very complex form of rhythm tap, I became more aware of what I did not know. What I performed and knew intuitively, I had never scrutinized with conscious appraisal. By convincing me of my talent and innate ability to swing, the masters of rhythm tap had relieved me of the responsibility of understanding what I was doing.

From 1973 to 1975, anticipating and helping to initiate the revival of tap dance, I began to present Honi Coles and members of the Copasetic Club to the students and audiences in New Paltz, at the college and at my own studio. It was there in 1975 that I produced and directed them in a two-hour documentary. *Great Feats of Feet: Portrait of the Jazz Tap Dancer* featured Honi Coles along with the dance comedy team of Cook and Brown, who were vaudeville stars as well as a specialty dance act in the original cast of *Kiss Me Kate* on Broadway. Brownie was the master of the pratfall, and their act consisted of Cookie appearing to beat on poor Brownie until he fell down. Interspersed with this shocking visual effect were their dances "The Big Apple," "The "Suzie Q," and the rhythms beaten out with their

Cookie Cook, Honi Coles, Bubba Gaines, and Buster Brown performing the Chair Dance in Great Feats of Feet.

canes to "Old Man Time." After the tap revival Cookie put taps on his shoes and created beautiful *soft shoe* routines which he taught to the next generation of dancers.

Leslie "Bubba" Gaines was with them, dancing a great rhythm solo and at the age of sixty-four still *doing the rope* (tapping with a jump rope) as he had when he performed with The Three Dukes in the 1940s. He had just come off a USO tour, and his feet were clean and articulate as he danced in a great circle, clicking his heels while lifting his hat high in the air. Bubba always finished his act with his tap dancing jump rope routine. When the audience began to howl with excitement after one chorus, he stopped and said, "If you keep encouraging me like this I'll completely destroy myself." Then he yelled to the band, "Takin' off fellas, down to the runway and here we go." He tapped the last chorus double time while the audience screamed and jumped to their feet. After taking a short bow he bounded from the stage and then ran back for his standing ovation.

Buster Brown, short, fast, and flashy, began his career in Baltimore. His syncopations were surprising, often ending with a gyration into a *snake hips* phrase and an unexpected drop into a split after a fast and low-to-the-ground *over the top*. Especially for the documentary he was joined by Albert Gibson, of the dance comedy team The Chocolateers, in a fabulous duet to "Breaking in a New Pair of Shoes."

James "Stump" Cross, the Stump of Stump & Stumpy, also a comedy dance team that headlined the vaudeville circuit, was master of ceremonies for the two-hour concert that we filmed along with classes and interviews. These dancers had given up hope of tap ever returning, but they kept their chops together performing in an occasional jazz festival and in the annual Copasetic Ball.

The Copasetic Club was created in 1949 in honor of Bill "Bojangles" Robinson, who coined the expression "Everything is copasetic." At one time Bill Robinson was the highest paid, best loved, and most respected black performer in show business. Throughout the interviews and during performances, the dancers paid him tribute. They told endless stories about the neatness of his taps and his fastidious closet of suits, hats, and shoes that matched. They told of the many benefits he performed that made him an honorary fireman and policeman (with a gold pistol) and gave him the prestigious honor of throwing out the first ball at a Yankee game in Yankee Stadium. And most impressive, Bill Robinson had the biggest funeral New York City had ever seen.

Honi had recreated and rearranged some of Bojangles' classic steps and composed a recitative, "The Mayor of Harlem was a dancin' man, he ruled the people with his shoes," which he performed a cappella before dancing to Uncle Bo's signature music, "Doin' the New Low Down." When Honi finished, he took a bow, lifted his derby, and said, "That was Uncle Bo, now this is me," and danced his amazing rhythm *time steps* with pant legs swinging over his long limbs. The audience held its breath not to miss a note from his fabulous feet.

The Copasetics were like the pied pipers of New Paltz; as they walked through town everyone waved or yelled hello and welcome. My friend Susan Slotnick, the exercise teacher at The Dancing Theatre, and her husband, Sam, made a barbecue in their backyard. After feasting on the chicken and organic greens, the Copasetics played darts and sang a ditty when Susan presented them with a chocolate, white-frosted tap-shoe cake, created by a local jeweler, Tom Ambosina. Bubba was especially pleased by this. "You mean we have to eat our shoes, taps and all," he said. Every night we enjoyed a sumptuous repast, delivered by four of five friends from town who joined us at the table and cleaned up all the mess afterward.

During the filming of *Great Feats of Feet* (and the festivals that followed) we noticed that many of the older dancers placed their imprint or footprint on a tune. Buster Brown was identified with "Cute" and "April in Paris." No one ever danced their solos to "A Train" or "Lady Be Good"; those were Chuck Green's tunes. Leon Collins became famous for his performance to "Flight of the Bumble Bee."

This week of immersion in tap dance was accompanied by my own return to the jazz standards and tunes I sang in clubs when I was seventeen: sad songs like "Little Girl Blue," "Angel Eyes," and "Lush Life" or bright openers like "I Like the Likes of You" or Fats Waller's upbeat "Don't Let it Bother You." "Just Friends" became one of my first signature pieces and my favorite swing tap number.

Nobody slept during that intense week of video taping workshops, interviews, and performances by these masters. We danced throughout the night under the low ceiling of my old red house across from a horse farm. Cookie, who talked so fast he stuttered, told stories by candlelight that no one understood, but we laughed until our sides ached anyway. Honi *sand danced* in the living room while Cookie played drumsticks on the top of the piano. Bubba played his trumpet while he taught my son Zach to play "In The Mood" on his saxophone.

Cookie, Buster, Brownie, Bubba, and Honi slept in my three extra bedrooms. Jane Goldberg, visiting for the event, slept on a cot in a little cubby at the top of the stairs, and Dorothy Wasserman, my assistant director, pitched a tent outside in the backyard. And we all danced until we dropped. I was transfixed and reinspired by the depth and complexity of this art form. I was overwhelmed with the generosity of the Copasetics but awed by how much I had yet to learn about rhythm tap and its presentation. After they left and the house echoed with rhythms and laughter, I tried to dance but couldn't. Every step sounded coarse and simplistic, repetitive and dull. I took off my shoes and sorrowfully placed them in the back of the closet, never to see daylight again.

After a few weeks a resolve broke through my malaise. I would practice as many hours, for as many years as it would take, to develop the refinement in my feet that I had been privileged to document during that miraculous week. I decided then to dedicate the rest of my life in dance, choreography, teaching, and performance solely to the development, preservation, presentation, and performance of tap dance.

(Refer to the documentary *Great Feats OF Feet*.)

FOUR

~

Finding the Choreograpic Voice

HONI LIKED TO RIDE the Adirondack Trailways to New
Paltz to watch me teach my classes, and create choreography for my company and myself. We were preparing for
our first performance with my company, which would take
place in the spring of 1978 in New Paltz, and at The Pilgrim Theater in New York City. Honi would sit in the
dark of the Old Main Building and watch quietly, saying
nothing. After a few months he finally offered, "I don't
know why you aren't incorporating your other dance styles
into your tap dance."

I had always kept them separate, as if the Afro-Cuban
dancer, the jazz dancer and the tap dancer had different
names. When Honi suggested something to me I immediately examined it for its value – positive or negative. The
magic of videotape offered me the perfect opportunity to
observe myself, and I found that he was exactly right.
Unfortunately that didn't make actually bringing my selves
together any easier. I had the vernacular moves, I just
couldn't find the way to integrate them into my taps. As
the weeks continued I made great efforts to incorporate

my other dance styles into my tap choreography; after every session I asked Honi if I had done it yet. He simply shook his head and muttered, "Nope."

The breakthrough came when I was singing and choreographing my original tune "Flame." By singing the song first and deeply penetrating the lyric, the image held while I danced the rhythms. My body wanted to tell the story with my taps – the hips moving, shoulders moving, even the head accenting the beats.

> *I've been a flame that flickers all through the night*
> *The moving darkness never puts out my light*
> *Flicker Flicker Flicker Flicker*
> *Try to put me out*
> *You'll burn your . . . burn your hands. . . .*

As I was dancing Honi came to the stage, sat down at the piano, and accompanied me. After the dance came to a close, he snapped the cover over the keyboard. "That's it!" he said, and never came back to the Old Main to watch another class or practice session again.

Finding your voice or your style is a very mercurial and illusive process. It would be more appropriate to say, "How can I get out of my own way, so my voice can find me?" If I'm looking for my voice, it's bound to hide or tighten up or start coughing. I have to loosen the ties that bind me – the constructs of historical opinion, the identification with other dancers' styles, and the preconceived notions of the public. All of these considerations hinder the investigation, starve the imagination, and embarrass the intuition.

It is a search for authenticity. What is authentic is what is happening now. A style brought forward from the distant past may be traditional or a tribute, but it is not authentic. It's fun and educational to learn and perform traditional dances, but they should also be used to help inform me of the possibilities and tools to use for my own unique composition. Discovering my voice comes with the insight a moment brings while looking at a bird in flight, a Picasso painting, a waterfall, my first grandchild, or listening to a Charles Mingus score. The depth of my experiences calls my voice to sing out to me.

Choosing Music and Creating Repertoire

The music we choose for our dances says something about us as a person as well as an artist. As situations and circumstances change, songs take on new meanings, cry out to be sung, to be danced.

When I was a little girl during the war, Mom was off to work at the fruit stand and Daddy was in Okinawa. I was home alone many days reading through my mother's "fake book," a book of popular songs that out-of-work musicians illegally copied. They wrote out the melodies with chord changes and bound them in a loose-leaf notebook. Many singers and musicians were thrilled to own one. They were very expensive.

My mother's "fake book" had one thousand tunes. I would learn one a day, plunking out the melody with my right hand and memorizing the lyrics. Nowadays this "fake book" is called the "real book," and going through the "real book," singing the songs, is still one of my favorite pastimes. Choosing new repertoire has the excitement of new beginnings.

1978: The Dancing Theatre Company Repertoire

When creating new work for my Dancing Theatre Company to perform, I returned to the swing standards that I danced and sang in my early career. This time I could create arrangements from the experience of so many years working in a variety of modes and genres.

Instead of creating short routines, I was creating suites of dances for me and Dancing Theatre Company members Dorothy Anderson, Bonnye MacCleod, and Pat Giordano. I needed songs and arrangements that complemented each other in a medley. Dorothy had found a very haunting, very slow version of "A Train," played by its pianist-composer Billy Strayhorn. His romantic interpretation set my imagination running. He treated the tune in a very open fashion, almost rubato, but with arpeggios and phrases that embellished and brought new life to the melody. I began my tap composition with that same premise, slow and open, with pauses, a flurry of taps, and then a sustained developed phrase. The band laid out after sixteen bars while we tapped an a cappella counterpoint section that built in tempo. We concluded abruptly and then returned to a slow *soft shoe* tempo as the band came in on the bridge. The chorus ended with the traditional "A Train" ending articulated by the taps. To give the piece a flourish of a finish I used multiple spins with a piano arpeggio and a drumroll.

After "A Train" we went directly into Dizzy Gillespie's "Night in Tunisia" at a very bright tempo. We began the dance with claps while improvising Latin body postures and moves. We tapped walking riffs on the swing section

of the music, danced the last sixteen bars of the chorus
with very syncopated staccato phrases, and finished with a
sharp flap and no tag at the end of the melody.

"Just Friends" was the last tune of the medley. We
opened with an a cappella *time step* in counterpoint. Each of
us took short solos, danced two bright, choreographed
choruses, and closed with a long exit step.

For an encore to this section we returned with an a cappella military, building to a three-point counterpoint and
ending with hornpipe rhythms to Charles Mingus's "Nos-
talgia in Times Square." Dorothy Wasserman and Pat
Giordano were the dancers in this suite. A third dancer was
needed to make the counterpoint sections ring, and that
had to be me, breaking my rule of never dancing with my
company. Since I was a soloist and an improviser, these
were the first dances I ever put to memory and performed
in ensemble.

On opening night at The Pilgrim Theatre on 3rd Street
between Avenues B &C in New York City, I was choked
with anxiety. I had been warned that it would be pretty
hard to get an audience to attend a dance concert in the
dilapidated and dangerous Alphabet City. To keep my
nerves in check I cleared debris from the front of the theater, and pushed an old mattress, parts of a refrigerator,
and broken chairs into the empty lot next to the theater,
noticing that my name on the marquis shone too brightly
against the gray tenements. To my surprise, as I was sweeping and struggling to get a cap back onto a burgeoning
hydrant, cabs began to pull up, and I rushed to the stage
door to ready myself to face a full house of an extremely
curious and enthusiastic public.

The dance that challenged me emotionally, intellectually, and technically that evening was the *soft shoe* "Taking A Chance on Love." This was a rendition of the signature piece by Coles and Atkins that Honi rechoreographed for Coles and Bufalino. It was famous for being the slowest dance ever created. It was so slow that the musicians had trouble holding down the tempo. It's a dance that required absolute control and balance: the ability to wait and wait and wait and then anticipate. Honi's trademark was going from single time into triplets, back to single time, and into double time. His dances, though often only one chorus, were filled with surprises. You could never anticipate where they were going to end up.

When the great acts like Coles and Atkins performed in theatrical houses like the Apollo Theater, the orchestra was in the pit in front of the dancers. For our concerts we placed the piano, drums, and bass to our right, downstage center. We wanted them close to us. This was the first time a tap dance company performed ensemble work on the concert stage and the first time Coles and Bufalino were on stage together. I never knew how tall he was . . . and how small I was . . . how small I could feel until my first performance with Honi Coles.

"Taking a Chance on Love"

Ohhhhh . . . this is not the way I dreamed it. Here I am in front of a thousand people dancing this classic *soft shoe* with the Great Honi Coles.

So where's the epiphany? Why aren't I floating on a bubble of euphoria?

Yes, I am lifting my leg. Yes, I am counting off the tempo . . . 1 2 1234.

Yes, I'm smiling.

Do I look beatific, as if I'm dancing next to God?

No! I'm shrinking. Every moment disappearing beneath the blinding light of his charisma.

Yes, my feet are hitting the floor, metal against wood.

But I can't hear the sound of my taps.

I can only hear the ringing in my ears.

He's never danced on stage with a woman before. And he's so tall. He has to look down on me.

I'm looking at him, but now he's ignoring me.

Oh no, I messed up that phrase. Now I've missed the entrance to the double time.

Breathe . . . Breathe

Do I look relaxed?

He always looks relaxed. But he's not relaxed at all. His energy is paralyzing me.

The critics have all picked up their tickets. They're out there writing that I'm white and young and blond.

Don't let them know how you feel, Bufalino.

Grow damn it grow. Take up space.

Either blow out his light or make your own light brighter.

All right . . . here comes that double shuffle. Hit it strong! But don't get too loud.

Is this one-chorus dance ever going to end? It feels like it's four choruses.

Breathe . . . Breathe

OK, here comes the triplet. Easy now . . . smooth. Let it be smooth.

Brenda Bufalino and Honi Coles dancing the soft shoe "Taking a Chance on Love."

They're all out there waiting for me to fail. No one wants me to win this one.

But he does. That's why he's dancing with me and not with them.

That's why they hate me.

Here comes the last double time with the break. It's over. Wow, it's over

Now he's taking my hand for the bow. He's smiling at me. He says, "You danced your can off."

~

FIVE

Collaboration & Confrontation

The Morton Gould Tap Concerto

IN THE WINTER OF 1979 Honi would often come up to my home in the country to practice and rehearse our shows in the quiet of my mountaintop retreat on Sparkling Ridge Road outside of New Paltz. The chalet was all stage set and no substance. It was bitterly cold and banks of snow blocked the steep quarter-mile driveway to my house. Honi's trousers were always well-pressed, and his shoes shined brightly wherever he went. On these snowy days his leather soles were like skis. Holding onto each other, we slid four steps backward for every six steps forward.

It was so cold in my living room that our breath created frost on the windows as we danced beside the potbelly stove with our gloves and hats on. We were creating the choreography for *The Morton Gould Tap Dance Concerto*, which was to be performed with the Brooklyn Academy Philharmonic. Originally composed for Paul Draper, it was subsequently performed by Danny Daniels. We were the first artists to perform the *Concerto* as a duet.

As Mr. Gould had written a tap dance score that did not always correspond to the way a tap dancer composes, the work was arduous and tedious. Except for the open cadenza, which Honi could choreograph with eight bar phrases, there were no other logical bar sequences. I was responsible for creating choreography to the classical structures unfamiliar to Honi. I followed Mr. Gould's written tap score closely until I was confident I understood his intention. Then I proceeded to invent my own rhythms and patterns to which I knew Honi could move easily. It was essential to memorize every phrase the orchestra played so that we could enter into our sequences at the right moment, and together. The musicians could play with the music in front of them, but we had to dance with the notes in our heads.

We wanted the concerto to look natural and have a sustained vitality. When the score didn't call for taps we kept dancing silently to keep the flow and visual excitement. James Levine, the conductor, decided to perform only three of the four *Concerto* movements. Honi opened with the Pantomime as a solo, and I followed solo with the Minuet. We performed the Tocatta together, breathing as one, listening for each other's sound, gesturing together with one voice. When the orchestra silenced for the Cadenza, free at last, our taps exploded like thunder building to a crescendo calling the orchestra back in for the final movement. The audience was moved to tears by the accumulated intensity of the performance and was certainly convinced by its impact that tap dance was indeed an art form with emotional as well as melodic and rhythmic dimension.

Tapestry

It is 1981 and I have come down off the mountain to live in a little cabin surrounded by pine and cedar trees. The front window faces the mountain, and my musings project off the shining granite face of the Shawangunk range. The dances are coming fast and furious now. Choreography surges up in me, haunts my dreams, and eagerly waits to find itself on the stage. It hardly seems a moment after the first idea hits for a counterpoint or a phrase before it is actualized in one of my solos or on my students.

Our 1978 performance of *Singin', Swingin' and Wingin'* with guest artist Honi Coles in New York City is long gone, and Dancing Theatre Company members Dorothy Wasserman and Bonnye MacCleod have moved on. Now it's just Pat Giordano and me. I am creating a forty-five-minute duet for us called *Tapestry* to be included in future concerts that also include Honi. The necessity for creating this epic choreography is twofold. It was initiated by Honi after I suggested that his short dances might be extended so that people could appreciate his remarkable footwork and phrasing.

He said, "That's ridiculous. People can tell if you can dance in one chorus."

I replied, "The idea isn't to prove you can dance, the idea is to create a piece of art."

He suggested curtly, "If you want to see a long tap dance then you make it. But I'm warning you, the audience will never sit still for it."

Arguments about the form and content of tap dance with my mentor, Mr. Coles, often ended up with either of us trying to prove the other wrong and oneself right.

Dorothy Wasserman, Brenda Bufalino, and Pat Giordano in Singin', Swingin'
and Wingin', *New York City, Pilgrim performance, 1978.*

Because he said I couldn't or shouldn't, I was determined to create a tap dance with an extended form of variations which people would not only sit still for but stand up for at its conclusion.

I also had a personal and secret incentive. I wanted to develop more finesse and refinement. I wanted to challenge my poor memory. It has always been my logic that the way to conquer a particular handicap or discharge a phobia is with a grand gesture. I give myself so monumental a task that by succeeding with it I will conquer all small things in the future with ease. The choreography for *Tapestry,* a forty-five-minute a cappella duet, came about in just such an ambitious climate of doubt and fear; it took over a year to complete.

To test audience stamina and endurance for sustained performance, Pat and I initially performed this duet in ten-minute sections. Performing short sections helped build our stamina for forty-five minutes of nonstop tapping.

The piece built slowly, opening with walking rhythms and short punctuated phrases that built into counter-rhythms and broke off into indeterminate irregular patterns that allowed us to enter into new tempos and time signatures. As a centerpiece I created syncopated movement without taps to give the audience a breath of silence. After each of us took our solo with the other dancer holding backup patterns, simultaneous improvisations led up to a fast *double time* closing.

As expected, when we finally premiered the entire forty-five minute piece at the Klinert Gallery in Woodstock, New York, the audience became restless after the traditional five minutes when a tap routine usually ended. Then, to our surprise, they settled back and allowed the rhythms to wash over them for the next forty minutes and finally rose to a standing ovation as the last pattern drew the odyssey to a close. *Tapestry* remains one of the most successful works I have created.

Sounds in Motion

Honi has finally forgiven me for having such a success with *Tapestry* and has come up to the country to rehearse our new show, *Sounds in Motion*. The big white Masonite tap boards cover the whole floor of my cabin in the valley. We have space to stretch out, and it's not as cold as on the mountaintop.

We are assembling a medley of our original songs into a set entitled "The Marital Mess" or "Connubial Chaos." Charlie Knicely, our bass player contracted on a yearly basis with funds from President Carter's CETA project, has made arrangements of Honi's tunes: "I Did It So What, I Fell In Love," "No Matter What You've Done I'll String Along," "The Doggonest Feeling Ever," "Get Yourself Another Guy," and of course, the ever favorite "I Was Alone When I Met You . . . Now I Wish I Was Alone."

In response to his songs are my original tunes, "Just Hit It," "What's It Like to Be Home Again, With a Girl of Your Own Again," "I've Been a Flame," and "No One There At All."

Honi prefers comedy to all else. To get a laugh he'll sell any ballad down the river by putting a quip at the end. For instance, at the end of his tender ballad "Get Yourself Another Guy," he smiles impishly and says, "And I'm available." And as for myself, I have my share of sarcastic wit to throw back when I'm not being a Gracie Allen type straight woman to his George Burns presentation.

The remarkable and often beautiful collaborations of Honi Coles and Brenda Bufalino were always developed from argumentative discourse, our primary source of entertainment when we weren't in tap shoes. Through our intense artistic dialogues we found a synthesis in the most unlikely places. Both of us enjoyed writing and performing monologues. When Honi was performing on tour with *Bubblin' Brown Sugar* he portrayed the great humorist Bert Williams, who would perform in blackface the famous card game and recitative "I Ain't Goin' to Do Nothin' for Nobody No Time." I had recently come across a George M. Cohan monologue, "Life's a Very Funny Proposition After All," created in 1904 for *Little Johnny Jones*, the Broadway play about a jockey who went to London to ride a pony. In our concert we performed these monologues in tandem. They seemed to portray the soul of the variety, vaudeville, and performance artists interpreting the life around them and also spoke of the very intense philosophies that Honi and I shared when we faced the world both separately and together.

Honi's temper would flare when he perceived himself caught in a racial stereotype, and he never allowed his work to succumb to the expected cliché. I was very sensitive to gender and racial exclusions, often confronting precious ideas of authenticity or appropriation in my original monologues. Honi argued that you could never beat the system or public consensus. His favorite saying was "Water finds its own level." Yet, in spite of himself, his imagination, artistic curiosity, and integrity often took him into uncharted tap territory. In contrast to Honi's professed laissez-faire attitude, I was always making dams, building bridges, or stomping on the concrete of solidified perceptions. He helped me to relax and temper my intensity with humor and contemplation. I agitated, pushed, and insisted that he keep coming into the studio for another practice.

Our approach to composition and choreography was consistent with the times we created in. Even in the 1980s Honi still held onto the constructs he understood so well from vaudeville and television: a dance should be short, sweet, and to the point. He was an absolute perfectionist. Each step of his one-chorus routine would be changed many times before it settled into its rightful place in the dance. And, very emphatically, he thought that I should use tunes that everyone knew and could identify with. Maybe a tune like "Sweet Sue" that any band could play with ease.

I, on the other hand, wanted to stretch my compositional skills and wanted the audience to stretch with me. I rarely changed a step; I just added another step or threw out an entire dance if one figure displeased me. I felt that my first instinct was the best, rarely challenged my first thought, and sought unusual music that would challenge me and the musicians I worked with.

Though I argued my point of view courageously and obstinately, I secretly and intently studied his approach. I saw that within the short time frame of one chorus he managed to develop very consistent and unique compositions filled with surprise. He never used flash in an isolated way but rather incorporated speed and physical daring into his syncopated phrasing. He never substituted flash for elegance and sophistication. Though our desired aims were often diametrically opposed, I admired his work more than that of anyone else I had ever known. I was his student, after all, and remained so until he died.

SIX

~

Crossfire & Counterpoint

A Segue

IN 1980, AFTER SIX YEARS, I began to feel abused working as an adjunct professor at SUNY New Paltz. Financially it kept me poor and tied to the university, while offering no health benefits or prospects for advancement. My hopes for the creation of a separate line for "Musical Theatre/ Jazz/Tap Dance" were dashed and trashed by the introduction of the new conservative administration. At the same time, a fitness center opened on Main Street, attracting my students to its machines and promise of easy weight loss. Classes at my studio were getting smaller even as my work was becoming more technically demanding. So I took all the touring work I could find, beating out of the bushes students who really wanted to work at learning, students who would practice and invent and who could articulate my rhythmic patterns.

After Dorothy and Pat quit and my Dancing Theatre Company dissolved, I realized I needed dancers who would stay around for a while, who did not have ambiguous ambitions and really wanted to be professional. Because I prided myself on being a rural artist, I had come home to the mountains after the big success at the Pilgrim instead of staying and working my hit show that could still be running on 3rd Street. But now the city was calling me, and Honi was calling me. "You've got to come out of those mountains, you're going to get buried up there. Move into the city, we'll teach together, maybe we'll open a studio together."

Only my dancing feet wanted to move to the city. My heart, my mind, and the rest of my body couldn't bear the thought of not waking up to the silver ridge of the Shawangunks sparkling through my cabin's window. But my children were grown, gone, didn't need me any more, and I was getting weary of worrying about frozen water pipes in New Paltz, while teaching and creating choreography in towns and cities I had never heard of before.

I would have to give away my Plumb Cat, the furry gray feline that closed her ears with her paws whenever I practiced my taps, that sat on my lap when I tried to play the piano, that hid under the bed when I practiced scales on my concertina. Fluffy Felicia Plumb, my guardian, my sole companion on snowy nights, who earned her keep keeping my house clean of varmints and who guarded my porch like a German shepherd.

And the big cedar tree, home of blue jays and squirrels, would have to give shade to an empty house. And the green pond, home of big, slimy frogs and the occasional blue heron, would have to stay clean without my sweeping the algae twice a week with a fish net.

I began slowly, subletting first at Westbeth, in the Village, and then I took a fifth-floor flat on 3rd street for a summer. And there were more sublets and more . . . small ones with no heat, big ones with too much heat, but never for more than a month or two.

When I was traveling back and forth on the Adirondack Trailways bus to New York City, my heart beat with both anxiety and anticipation. This was indeed a segue . . . choreography for the vagabond.

Bufalino & Company

Tap dance marched into the 1980s on a drumroll of expectation and anticipation. Honi and I traveled often to Portland, Oregon, teaching and performing. Somehow, in Portland they never realized that tap had died. At Jefferson High School we found many excellent teachers and tappers like Bev Mellum and Deb Brozka. Their students were eager for our material. The Jefferson Dancers commissioned me yearly to create new work. Directed by Mary Folberg, this semiprofessional company of high school and college alumni members toured regularly throughout Portland, Oregon, and Washington State. On consecutive tours to Portland Honi and I performed *Sounds in Motion* as well as *The Morton Gould Tap Concerto,* and on our final visit the rest of the performing Copasetics also joined us for a short tour of the Northwest. Over the years, sharing the stage with these master practitioners of the joyful art of tap dance, I became reacquainted with the entertainer I had been as a small child, the performer who loved to make an audience happy.

I returned to New York City determined to integrate the joy and traditions of the masters into my work, while creating new forms of tap choreography that would also place demands on audiences who, when they heard about a concert of tap dance, thought only of Shirley Temple and Bojangles or Fred Astaire and Ginger Rogers.

After two years of training, the dancers in my city class were gaining expertise and accumulating my material. A small group consisting of Jackie Raven, Kathryn Kramer, Lynn Jassem, Ann Amendologine, Trina Marx, Debbie Robertson, Anita Feldman, and Neil Applebaum magnetized into my first New York ensemble, Bufalino & Company. We traveled back and forth to Boston, performing and exchanging energy with Leon Collins and his students.

Leon, a virtuoso tapper, was one of the casualties of the tap demise. With no more performance jobs Leon went to work simonizing cars, where he lanquished until C. B. Heatherington, Pam Raff, and Dianne Walker created a tap scene and studio for him in Boston. He was dancing better than ever with his "angels," as he called them. Leon approached his compositions with clear and understandable phrasing of crisp straight eighth notes accented and syncopated by clapping sections, quick turns, and sharp angular movements. Even in performance he dutifully executed on the left and right side. This gave his performance a certain predictability and satisfying comprehensibility.

Finally, with the exception of Ann and Trina, who had moved on, "Bufalino & Company" prepared a concert for the Theater at Riverside Church. For this concert, besides swing and blues numbers, I created my first a cappella piece for large ensemble. I have manipulated and reinvented this piece in a variety of contexts ever since.

The name "Crossfire" seemed to explain the way I used counter rhythms in 4/4 time with a segue into a Latin merengue tempo and mode, then into a robust 6/8, and concluding with patterns in 10/4. The counterpoint in this piece was intense and dramatic. It proved to me that a standard for a powerful counterpoint that is viscerally exhilarating depends on the many rhythms forging finally into one, just as in life we live in many realities simultaneously.

I studied *Crossfire* for many years after it was completed and finally was able to make conscious what had come to me intuitively: *It is even more imperative in a counterpoint for the toe to be the melody and the high notes and the heel to be the bass and low notes. A strong bass heel is what integrates the multiple rhythms laying over each other. Without a strong bass heel all those rhythms together would just sound like clatter.*

For the Riverside Theater concert I interspersed tap compositions between stanzas of my three-part recitative.

First Stanza
That's Jazz then . . . listening
  Corresponding interplays of sound and silence
  A hot breath on a cool phrase
  A syncopated throbbing of a deep hidden primordial memory
High weeds . . . hot sun . . . rain

Second Stanza
Or a city
A city waking on a hazy blue morning
Hurried sounds whisper as shadows play against the empty street
Doors open . . . Windows open . . . Motors running . . . People
  running
What's the time . . . what's the time
People walking . . . People walking . . . That's Jazz

Third Stanza
A woman is jazz that's why men dance it and men play it
Play the rhythm to her melody

A woman is jazz
Like a boat is a woman
Like a woman is a plane
Like a woman is a flame

I have always included narratives and vocals in my concerts. My voice sings my feet, the taps tell the story.

Production Values and Amplification

When I was touring with Honi or The Copasetics and the lighting technician asked about our requirements, Honi would always say, "Give us red, white, and blue and make it bright." If there was a standing microphone on stage, the dancers avoided it, and the taps were usually drowned out by the drummer. A tap dance act in vaudeville or variety never had to consider lights or sound, but ensemble tap for the concert stage in the early 1980s was a brand new form. Atmosphere was required, a composition could be moody or subtle requiring a varied light plot, or the lights could emphasize a buildup in rhythmic dynamics.

I was not interested in a precision tap line like the Rockettes, where all the dancers did the same step and created intricate kick-line formations, or a tap chorus line that opened and closed a variety show with flashy steps and bright costumes. *Crossfire* was a musical and rhythmic composition that asked the audience to use their ears even more than their eyes. Suddenly it was necessary to have a good sound system. In my work, every tap dancer needed to be heard. Each section of a counterpoint needed to be equal in volume to the other four or five sections. The struggle that I had convincing a soundman to provide microphones for tap was a forecast of the deep and enduring problem of presenting tap with live music on the concert stage where dance had previously been accompanied only by canned taped music.

The technical needs of the tap dancer are very specific. We need microphones, preferably shotguns with a wide range of tonality. PCCs or PCM "pick-up" microphones should only be used as a boost for presence. We also need monitors so that we can hear our taps in relationship to the rest of the band, and our taps need to be in the band's monitor so they can hear us and we don't loose track of each other. In the early years of the tap renaissance, sound technicians on every job were extremely resistant to thinking of taps as instruments. We needed to be very insistent; encouraging them to listen carefully, convincing them that just because they could see the rhythm didn't mean they were hearing all of it.

~

SEVEN

The White Tuxedo:
At the Village Gate

ALL THE GREATS WERE TO BE ON THE BILL in New York City at The Village Gate in the early 1980s: Bubba Gaines, Cookie Cook, Chuck Green, Honi Coles. And then me . . . replacing Bunny Briggs.

I was the only female dancer on the bill, and I was standing in for a top tap star. After I accepted this gig I felt as if I were traversing where there were land mines or tapping my way into a giant sinkhole that would swallow me up. My reviews for "Bufalino & Company" at the Riverside Theater had been overwhelmingly positive, but I wondered, "Has anyone read those reviews, does anyone know who I am?" Yes, I had a following, a really devoted community of fans, but they were up in the mountains bathing in the ice-cold streams of the Shawangunks . . . stark naked.

"The audience expects Bunny Briggs, they don't expect me." I thought. "Nor will they be pleasantly surprised when they hear my name."

Honi suggested I dance my jazz waltz for contrast. "You know Buff, show the versatility of tap dance, show its feminine side."

"Oh fine," I thought. "He always wants me to do my waltz and show my feminine side."

Well, it was a very good waltz, lyrical, but with long and unexpected melodic phrases, syncopated with accents hitting just before and after the beat, the taps gliding over the bar like taffeta over silk. And there was space between the beats for my arms to arc and sweep. Then, of course, making a nod to tradition, I would break into a *waltz clog* or a 3/4 repetitive step that propelled me around the stage in giant airy loops. It was at once regal and proud, then gentle. The last eight bars led gently into a vamp, softer and softer, almost like a whisper; then my hands caressed the band into silence, and I took a breath and tapped out a thundering arpeggio. But no matter how beautiful the dance, it was still a waltz, sweet and feminine. Everyone would relax. They wouldn't be on the edge of their seats like they would be for Bunny Briggs as he *paradiddled* with fluttery feet around the stage, occasionally jerking his knee up and down with a resounding syncopation.

Bunny was a constant surprise with his huge bunny eyes and his mop of shiny gray hair swinging from his left temple to his right as he jerked around to face the audience head on, insisting on applause. He was fast, his bebop phrasing like art deco filigree in motion.

I remembered the first time I saw Bunny Briggs on tape in 1977, when Jane Goldberg took me all the way up to Lake George to look at Ernie Smith's archival collection of tap dancers. This was vintage footage from the earliest days of film with many nameless dancers, some with names I'd never heard. But they were all male, definitely all male. In four hours of clips I saw Rubber Leg Holmes, Patterson and Jackson, the Step Brothers, the Berry Brothers, Buck and Bubbles, Chuck and Chuckles, Moke and Poke, and Hal Leroy. We saw one stylish dancer after another, including Bunny Briggs on a clip from the Ed Sullivan show. His hair was black then, and there was even more of it to shake around. His manicured hands danced around his gray zoot suit, and his feet sang phrase after phrase of uninterrupted bebop lines over the stop time the band was playing.

And then another man, and another man. In four hours, not a single female soloist or trio. "Where are the women?" I asked.

"There weren't any." Ernie replied. "Gene Kelly said it; "Tap dancing is a man's game altogether."

Even the critic Sally Sommers eventually wrote in a 1980 *Village Voice* article that women couldn't tap dance, especially white women. And here I was standing in for Bunny Briggs at the Village Gate, and Honi wanted me to do my waltz. "Well," I thought, "that would certainly keep me in my place."

"Oh God . . . what will I wear?" I wondered as I pulled everything out of my closet. "If Honi wants me to do my waltz, should I wear the white lace jump suit with the flowing sleeves that I wore when he and I performed the *Tap Dance Concerto?* No, no, no, that was a classical dance with a totally different crowd, a classical crowd. No, this is the first Downtown Jazz Festival. This will be a hip crowd; I can't wear the white lace. Well, how about my sparkling silver jumpsuit. That's pretty hip, but maybe too skimpy, too form-fitting. I certainly can't wear any of my beautiful dresses. I hung up my sequin gowns a long time ago. When

I put on those black oxford men's shoes, that was the end of the dresses."

I had gone into flat shoes right after my high-heeled black Beck's pumps broke in two from too much hard hitting and too much practice. I had had it with that ticky-tacky sound from my heels. And I didn't care any more what Honi thought or the other guys thought about how beautiful my legs looked in short skirts. I wanted to lay down the iron, get that bass note from my heel, and get some sound out of my damn shoes.

Honi had not been pleased about the shoes. He had purposely never let on that the shoe I was wearing could have any bearing on the way I tapped. I took a big risk, but the world heard the difference, and it wasn't long before all of my women students were changing their shoes. Soon Honi began singing a different tune when he saw a lady in her pumps. "She must not be serious," he would whisper to me.

I had won that battle but still received notices from the critics that although I could certainly dance, I didn't look like a tap dancer. So, the matter of what I would dance at the Village Gate to take Bunny's place got all tied up, like the knots in my shoelaces, with what I would wear.

I needed a new costume but I couldn't afford to have one made, and Lord & Taylor's or Bergdorf Goodman were definitely out of my reach. I thought I'd just walk down to 21st and Eighth Avenue and stop in at the Salvation Army. I looked through the jacket section, the jumpsuit section, even the lingerie section. Then I saw it right across from the black satin pajama set — a white, three-piece tuxedo. Oh, it was sharp, very tailored and cream colored, not too brash, not too white. The vest had three buttons, and the collar was stylish, the pants only slightly flared at the bottom. Would this fit me? I tried it on over my clothes between the jacket rack and the lingerie. It fit perfectly.

"How much is it?" I looked at the tag: $25. I can buy it.

I had $25, and I had white men's oxford tap shoes to go with the suit. "Do I dare, do I dare? Yes I do, yes I do."

When I got back to my sublet apartment I finally began to plan my dance set. The choice of my material was not a casual matter. I couldn't go on stage and wing it like I usually did. I had to think this through.

Finally, I decided to open my set casually, not look like I was trying too hard. Do a little walking dance to "Don't Get Around Much Anymore." And then go on from there to talk to the audience very casually about their disappointment over seeing me rather than Bunny Briggs. I would mention that we did have something in common, our initials were the same, we both had big smiles, and we wore the same size shoe. Then I would go into an edited version of my waltz. And just when the audience thought I was through, I'd do a fast three choruses of my best bebop to Charlie Parker's "Anthropology."

That would be an excellent set and it would be different. None of the guys danced to Charlie Parker tunes. They all danced to swing tunes, and after my waltz, it would be a big surprise.

The night of the gig, carrying my white tuxedo in a garment bag, I pushed through the line at the box office. The great black cavernous downstairs room of the Village Gate was already almost filled to capacity. Nodding and waving to familiar tap dancers who filled the first row, I circled around the small black Masonite stage and ducked behind the shredding black velvet curtain into the tiny dressing room. It was still musty and dusty from the powders and paint left behind by the last cast of *One Mo' Time*.

Honi and the guys were dressing in between the rows of olive oil and spaghetti sauce cans in the kitchen. "Fifty years of performing in jazz clubs, and the artists are still dressing in the kitchen," Honi mumbled.

As we lined up on stage left for our entrance in the "Walk Around," Bubba and Cookie just looked at me, sighed disgustedly, and said, "Well, if you're going to dress like us, at least wear a black tuxedo so you won't look like the star of the show."

It was the usual order. The "Walk Around" was the opener, with me, white girl in white tuxedo, coming on last. After the "Walk Around" we all demonstrated our *time steps*, with Cookie throwing his hat in the air and catching it every time he came to the break of the "Bambolina" *traveling time step*. Then, as usual, came "The Old Soft Shoe," and "The BS Chorus." Finally after Louie Simm's solo and Leroy Meyer's solo, it was my turn. I had the presence of mind to do just what I had planned. The audience was chilly at first, audibly disappointed. I didn't let the cool reception distract me. And sure enough, when I didn't push too hard and acknowledged their disappointment with comments about the similarities and disparities between Bunny Briggs and me, the audience took pity on me and laughed while they applauded. I did my waltz. It was just what they expected. I took my bow to polite applause and Honi bounded on stage. "Well let's have it for Brenda Bufalino. Even if she's in a white tuxedo she's still a lovely lady. What a beautiful waltz."

I turned abruptly, looked him straight in the eye, and said, "I'm not finished yet." Before he could say anything I counted in the band for my bebop. He stood on the side of the stage with his mouth hanging open. I could feel the fiery breath of his fury. But the audience was goading me on. They started yelling back at my punctuated phrasing, "We hear ya. Go get it." The dance was so fast that it was finished in a flash. But it was long enough for the audience to finally get it, forget about Bunny Briggs, jump to their feet and finally admit a woman could lay down the iron.

When Honi brought me back for my third bow his face was beaming with acknowledgment and relief. It wasn't necessary to protect me anymore. "She can take care of business," he said to the guys in the dressing room.

~

EIGHT

An Improvisation

on Tap Improvisation

IMPROVISATION IS A WAY OF LIFE. Some people like to know where they are going at all times and others only want to find out where they are going when they get there. Even as a young dancer in my family's act The Strickland Sisters, I had a terrible memory. Forgetting my steps as soon as I hit the stage, I improvised and used a lot of personality, energy, and expression so the audience wouldn't sense my panic. It was exhausting, but it was also exciting – always leaving the familiar, always leaving home base.

I also had a taste for fear and risk, generated perhaps by my mother's wish that I become independent at a very young age. Because my mother was always at least an hour late picking me up after class, I preferred to take the bus home. If I got off at the wrong stop, I would travel through the woods, in the dark, up to Banks Terrance. Finally, arriving at my grandmother's house for dinner, I was greeted with cold pot roast, string beans gone soggy from too long in the pot, and only a casual, unconcerned greeting. As no one in my family ever arrived anywhere on time, I guess they never realized I was continually lost. They expected me to be late and trusted that I would arrive home eventually.

My mother's philosophy of life was a formula for improvisation. "Always take risks. There's nothing to lose. The worst that can happen is that you end up back where you started." She was brave and stubborn and spent her life making something out of nothing. Swampscott was a well-to-do ocean suburb of Boston and we lived in its only slum: one tenement and a train station. Our stairs were crooked, the outside paint was peeling, the coal furnace rattled, and the floorboards looked like the waves rolling in on Fishermen's Beach. But Marjorie found discarded brocade fabrics and worked them over on the old pedal sewing machine until our little living room and bedrooms were padded and upholstered like a pasha's palace. Every night she would play jazz chords and fragments of melodies on our gilded gold upright piano to calm my spirits and hyperactive energies.

It was only natural and preordained, when I left home in my teenage years and wandered from club to club listening to big bands and small, that I would want to live in the world of jazz forever. I loved to hear the soloists improvise over the standards, and I had already memorized so many tunes that I, too, enjoyed playing one melody over another with my voice and my feet. I thought all dancers were, like me, improvising from scratch, just wailing off a tune in a constant state of invention. But I discovered years later that many dancers were only paraphrasing, by taking steps and realigning them, putting them in new contexts, or perhaps improvising a new ending for a composed eight-bar step.

Except for Baby Lawrence or Teddy Hale, most of the great masters did not believe in just getting on stage and winging it. Though they created their compositions through improvisations, their material was set. Musical arrangements accompanied every step, and were well rehearsed with the band. They refined their compositions and performed them with such finesse and ease that they always looked improvised.

When Jane Goldberg's Changing Times Tap Dance Company produced the 1980 "By Word of Foot" festival in New York City, she presented John Bubbles as a featured guest. Most tap dancers considered John Bubbles to be the father of rhythm tap. By dropping the heels for his bass notes, he created fresh, uncharted, and intricate syncopations. He also had an elegant and upright style with a smooth delivery. A singer and actor as well as a dancer, John Bubbles was the original Sporting Life in the Broadway production of *Porgy and Bess*.

When Jane interviewed Bubbles, we were all surprised to hear him say, "Improvisation is for the rehearsal hall. On the professional stage your material should be set."

But in the tap renaissance, improvisation was becoming an integral part of many performances. We were all leaving room for improvisation in our solos or choreography. So it was a fresh idea, perhaps not suitable for vaudeville, television, or the movies, but at the Colorado Tap Festival in 1986 and all the festivals thereafter we dancers were stretching out and performing longer solos, medleys, and a cappella improvisations. In the 1930s and 1940s elaborate arrangements played by a big band or orchestra sold the act; now we integrated ourselves into the musical ensemble of piano, bass, and drums, conducting them with our feet.

John Bubbles was from a different era, and a stroke had left him partially paralyzed and in a wheel chair. If he had been able to dance along with us in those early revival years, I wonder how his views might have adapted and developed. The rules have changed. Tap is not just show business any more; it is an art form with elastic boundaries. There is room and time on the concert stage to take risks and expand into the future while paying tribute to our traditions.

Now in the twenty-first century, following in the footsteps of Savion Glover, young dancers are jamming and ad-libbing with each other in great abandon, creating the extreme sport of tap dance. The audience has developed a taste and expectation for the risk and improvisational energy of this art form and will offer a new performer encouragement and permission to explore.

Some dancers know a few steps, a few patterns, and begin to experiment at a jam session, and some get jobs performing short routines for a delighted audience. But after a while they begin to wonder, "Shouldn't I be able to listen to the pianist or drummer when I'm improvising? Shouldn't I be able to hear the arrangements the band is playing on a compact disc while I'm dancing? Is there a way to be inspired by the music rather than just using it as a metronome?"

Being an ad-lib dancer is tricky business: here today, gone tomorrow. I've heard many dancers complain, "One night my feet might seem to fly; the next night they can't get off the ground, and somehow my improvisations seem as repetitious as my routines. Something is missing. It all seems the same. Is this all there is?"

Perhaps it's time to go back to the beginning to refine and define. "What is a *shuffle* anyway?" you wonder. "How can I do it better?" Then some new discoveries follow: "It's not all as simple as I thought." And then there are more discoveries, and more, and you finally realize that your feet are your instrument and the floor is a part of this instrument. Eventually, as you persist, you find yourself rapt in a unique phrase or breaking down the time against the rhythm, and there is discovery and excitement as you begin to hear your personal statement. When you are playing the floor with the feet, wonderfully, miraculously, that's all there is in the world.

NINE

The Broadway Tap Revival

WE WERE SITTING ON TWO STOOLS in a very cold loft I was subletting on 21st Street in 1982 when Honi told me the news. It was great news. It made me so happy for him, yet it was also bittersweet because I knew there would be no new shows for us. Our touring and dancing days together would be over. The choreographer-director Tommy Tune had offered him a role in *My One and Only*, a new show starring Tommy and Twiggy, with music by George Gershwin.

There was more good news; he had to make a choice, because he was also offered roles in two other new Broadway shows, *The Tap Dance Kid* and *Black and Blue*. Honi had played the uncle, one of the leads, in a made-for-television special of *The Tap Dance Kid*, which won a well-deserved Emmy. Now he was offered the part of a ghost, and Hinton Battle would play the uncle on Broadway. He didn't like that idea very much. He also didn't like the idea of going into the revised version of *Black & Blue*, which originally had a long run in France. The producers were looking for a choreographer who could create dances from the swing era in many different modes: *soft shoe, stair dance, swing dance.* They wanted him to choreograph as well as perform. Honi didn't like to choreograph so he recommended me, an idea they quickly rejected. This was an all-black show, and again I was Goldilocks in the house of the three bears. Honi also heard that the show was under an AGVA contract instead of the usual Equity contract, and that there was a lot of trouble backstage. It was said not to be a happy show, and Honi liked harmonious environments. On the other hand, he thought Tommy Tune was a gentleman and had good backing for his show, and that it wouldn't be too arduous, so he easily made the choice for *My One and Only.*

Honi loved working in Broadway shows. Even in his prime he had performed with his partner Cholly Atkins in *Gentlemen Prefer Blondes* and in a summer stock production of *Kiss Me Kate.* Then, suddenly, the demand for tap dance had ended. In 1959 he had retired his shoes and become the manager of the Apollo Theater.

But in 1974 he began touring on and off with *Bubblin' Brown Sugar.* Broadway was really heating up and beating with tap rhythms. The tap revival began with *Bubblin' Brown Sugar* and *No No Nannette* in the seventies and really took off in the eighties with the revival of *42nd Street, Eubie* (starring the Hines Brothers), *Sophisticated Ladies* (starring Gregory Hines), and now *The Tap Dance Kid, Black and Blue, My One and Only,* and the ill-fated revival of *Singing in The Rain* directed and choreographed by Twyla Tharp. Though Gower Champion was a great director, and Twyla Tharp was the director of a great modern dance company, neither was a tap dance choreographer. They worked in the grand tradition of Broadway productions, pasting together tap numbers from the steps contributed by the chorus line. Or like Agnes DeMille had done in *Gentlemen Prefer Blondes,* they had the tap dancers do their own choreography and get no credit in the program for their work. This was also the case in the original *Kiss Me Kate*, choreographed by Hanya Holm, where Cook and Brown created their own material, and in *Sugar*, directed again by Gower Champion, where Steve Condos happily choreographed the big tap number, "Tear the Town Apart," with no credits in the program and no extra money.

The Tap Dance Kid, however, would be choreographed by a real tap dancer, Danny Daniels, who was also creating dances for the movie *Pennies from Heaven*. Danny Daniels had a real choreographic voice, as did Tommy Tune. Though Tommy admitted he didn't know many steps, he had a definite choreographic tap style that incorporated the *tap Charleston*, and he could really move a tap chorus around the stage seamlessly with dynamic design. He also had the good sense to have Honi choreograph the number they sang and danced together to the title tune, "My One and Only." Unfortunately, Honi received no credit for choreography except for a slight mention in the back of the program, "Special material by Honi Coles." Honi didn't mind this omission. He was happy to be in a hit show; he loved going to work every night and, unlike myself, was delighted to dance the same dance every show.

For his part in this production Honi won a Tony Award for best supporting actor as well as the Fred Astaire Award, and the Drama Desk Award. Years later he proudly accepted the Medal of Arts Award from the first President Bush. It was a joy to see so many of his dreams realized later in life, especially as he had lost faith that tap dance would ever return to popularity. When I had suggested in 1973 that tap dance could be a concert form, that I wanted

to do a documentary on tap dance, and that he would be
the most significant voice in the tap revival, he had told me
he thought that was the dumbest thing he had ever heard.

All three of the shows Honi was offered were successful.
Black and Blue starred all the rhythm tap giants, among them
Jimmy Slyde and Bunny Briggs, with special choreography
by Cholly Atkins and the Nicholas Brothers. Frankie Man-
ning created the jazz chorus choreography and Henry
LeTang, the tap chorus choreography. Dianne Walker performed Cholly's *soft shoe* with a trio in the show and was the
rehearsal director for all the different choreographers. The
whole community was ecstatic that our style of tap was at
last represented on Broadway.   Danny Daniel's *The Tap
Dance Kid* launched the career of the young Savion Glover,
who was the first young man to star in the title role and
who went on to develop his own unique choreographic
voice on Broadway in *Bring in da Noise, Bring in da Funk.*

So now that musicals were singing again on Broadway,
the New York professional dancers were scurrying to learn
tap dance. If you could sing, walk, and chew gum at the
same time, looked the part, and could fit into the costume,
you could get a job tap dancing in the chorus on Broadway.
My classes at Steps Studios were filled with long-legged
dancers in high-heeled tap shoes who had never tapped,
didn't like tap dance, but wanted to learn *time steps* to audi-
tion for the shows.

I don't know why I was never interested in steady work.
How much easier my life would have been if I could have
taken direction from someone else. The only person I ever
trusted to direct me, other than Honi Coles, was Bill Irwin,
the comic genius, who was my tap student and in the early
1980s cast me as a tap dancing stenographer in his brilliant

production of *The Court Room* at St. Clemens Theater. After seeing Bill's production of *In Regard of Flight*, I would have felt honored to play any part he offered, and it was a joy watching his antics and those of the other main characters in the play: Bob Berky, Michael O'Connor, and the mesmerizing juggler Michael Moschen.

But my rightful place was in the concert world, writing my own material, creating my own dances, and building a company where tap dance would be appreciated as an art as well as an entertainment.

Coles and Bufalino performing in Blackpool, England, for Granada Television.

TEN

~

The Solo Show

WHEN I LEFT THE COUNTRY I left the source of my inspiration behind. The lichen-covered rocks, tall, wide-skirted maples and weeping willows had always whispered their poems to my pen and enticed a meditative and insightful state. In order not to leave completely, not to make a convulsive leap away from my Wallkill River muse, I kept subletting in New York. Every week for two years I carried suitcases stuffed with clean and dirty clothes, hair dryer, and home-cooked food up the long staircase to Fazil's on 46th Street where I was teaching my weekly classes. I tugged and pulled Masonite boards onto the Adirondack Trailways bus and unloaded them onto my little trolley at Port Authority, so I would have a floor to perform on at the Blue Note jazz club every fifth Monday night.

There is no more debilitating experience than looking for a cheap apartment in New York City. Desperate and exhausted from hauling stuff from the East Side to a new sublet on the West Side, I finally made the big move and gave up any idea of cheap. I rented a studio, duplex basement apartment over a boiler for $700 a month I couldn't afford. This apartment offered me so much wet heat that I had to keep the sole window open in February. It was located on Thompson Street, between West 3rd and Bleeker, one block away from the Blue Note, where I shared the stage with the Amy Duncan Trio every fifth Monday for an entire season. The stage was a three-by-four-foot wooden floor in front of the bandstand, flanked by two of my white Masonite boards.

Flash Cannielo was the agent and producer of these events. His black hair faced in all directions and his separated buckteeth protruded from a mouth that talked a lot of jive. In his platform shoes, high-water black trousers, and turquoise Florida shirt, he would introduce me: "On this particliur night, instead of our regliur show we have tap dance." We brought in a bigger crowd every performance. Flash loved our act, and I was grateful to him for giving tap dance a chance in such a prestigious club.

I loved creating choreography for my companies, but I liked to perform dances solo. I experienced the audience as my partner in the jazz atmosphere of the Blue Note. We were on a journey together, building slowly and intimately a relationship that became deeper as the hour progressed. Performing regularly with pianist-composer Amy Duncan, I could develop original dance, vocals, and monologues through improvisation ... spontaneously, in front of an audience. I always sought clues from my life when developing new material and examined my own history for universal parallels. Even as a child I often felt like Goldilocks finding herself in a house where she didn't belong, without a chair to fit into. I was often angry and frightened. Fortunately I found that fear and anger were powerful motivations, fueling my practice and innovation. To my surprise the anger and disappointment dissipated by the time the new material reached the stage, and my fury morphed into comedy.

By 1983 I had created my first all tap, one-person show, *Cantata & the Blues*, in response to the limitations and prejudices arbitrarily loaded onto the back of tap dance as well as the racial and gender stereotypes that choked each attempt at a revival. My interest was in experimentation, interpreting and intermingling vocals and taps with the autobiographical dramatic text. This show was also a tribute to my family and the freedom they allowed me, even as a child, to pursue my own course no matter how troublesome. Here is an excerpt:

> *My mother sang me the blues*
> > *She sang "Summertime" sweet and sorrowful*
> *She sang me hymns*
> > *She sang in church sometimes . . . sweet and joyful*
> *Bach and Count Basie*
> *Chopin and Ellington*
> *Gilbert & Sullivan and Cab Calloway too*
> *It was all the same to me*
> *Touched my heart*
> *Colored my skin every which way*
> *Freckle face and bucktoothed*
> *I didn't know I'd have to choose*
> *Between the Cantata & the Blues someday*

Amy wrote some beautiful music. I loved to dance a waltz to her "Waterways," after talking about my childhood, and then swing it into maturity when talking about life on 52nd Street. Her original tribute to Thelonious

Monk, "Monk Creeps In," was an investigation of changing meters, periodically knocking with three persistent taps
on the door to life.

I opened that show with my original monologue "In the
Beginning," followed by another original vocal, "This is
the Beginning." And I am still finding ways to work with
this material, and I am still singing and dancing "The Too
Tall Too Small Blues" about how it feels being a woman in
men's shoes.

I also sang and danced to a Billy Strayhorn medley,
"Lush Life," "Chelsea Bridge," and "Prelude to a Kiss," all
rubato, letting the taps string like ribbons of rhythm over
the sweet, sorrowful lyric and melody, finally jumping to
attention with syncopated alleluias on "Satin Doll." I am
still performing that one-person show more than twenty
years later, making additions when new events appear.
When my grandchildren were born I always received news
of their arrival in a different country. In order to keep them
with me in spirit, I still sing and dance to the wonderful
Thad Jones waltz "A Child is Born."

I've created and performed one-woman shows about
birds. My favorite is the dance story of *The Racing Pigeon*, in
which, while putting on her makeup at her dressing table,
the racer tells the audience about the arduous training she
endures for the glory of winning this race. She then puts on
her cape and races through the perilous storm, tapping to
the music of Ravel's Allegro. The woodpecker in *Journals of
a Woodpecker* introduces himself as the organizing principle
in the forest. This concept has had many incarnations. Due
to financial constraints, I even toured without live music, in
a piece called *Unaccompanied*, singing and dancing about the
lonely life of a minstrel with an interactive audiotape.

There is so much to sing and dance about if you let your story seep down to your shoes where the rhythm can shout it out.

One of the challenges in presenting a whole concert of original material is to let each dance have its own voice with each composition distinctively different from the one in front of it, varying tempos, modes, music, and harmonics as well as the emotional qualities. Each dance has its own reason for being, every step or figure true to the whole intention of the composition, each composition an integral part of the overall theme.

ELEVEN

~

The Tap Festivals

IN 1986 THE MODEL FOR BIG TAP FESTIVALS and reunions was
created by Marda Kirn, the director of the Colorado
Dance Festival, along with another champion of tap dance,
Sali Ann Kriegsman. Here master tap dancers could refine
the art of teaching their unique styles and celebrate the fine
art of tap dance. For this groundbreaking venture Sali and
Marda hired only the older black male artists to teach
classes and perform in their festival. Lynn Dally, Jane
Goldberg, and I were invited only to sit on panels and discuss the art of these elder statesmen.

Both Lynn Dally and I had companies and were recognized performers, producers, and teachers, and Jane Goldberg was also a teacher, dancer, and producer in her own
right. But at the time it did not seem fitting, or to use the
word of the day, "authentic," to Marda and Sali Ann to
have white women participating in the festival. Because of
our experience we were asked many of the how's and why's
of running a festival and were recognized for our contributions in bringing tap back into the forefront, but we were
not invited to perform or to teach. This presented a real

91

challenge for us. We, of course, wanted to participate in this grand first event, yet we were insulted by the prospect of contributing only our verbal understanding of the tap masters' styles. Even so we three decided to swallow our pride, paid our own way to the festival, and dutifully addressed the audience about the roots and development of tap dance.

At one of the panel discussions, a tap dancer and audience member, Terry Brock from Portland, Oregon, spoke up and said, "Why aren't these women teaching? They are our mentors!" Terry's sentiments were echoed by many others in the audience, but the producers hushed the questions. They said it was not appropriate to address this issue at this time.

The uproar over the controversy brought the news of our exclusion to Gregory Hines, who was a very influential leader in our community. The night of the performance, in the middle of his number, he yelled out, "Where are the women?" Gregory was like that, he didn't always anticipate an injustice or incongruity, but once he comprehended it he couldn't let this obvious injustice go unaddressed. He called Lynn, Jane, Dorothy Wasserman, Dianne Walker, and me up on the stage. I was wearing high heels and a tight skirt. I yelled out to Greg, "I don't have the right clothes." "Wait just a minute," he said, ran backstage and gave me his tap shoes and a pair of his pants to wear. They were both much too big, so I stuffed my socks in his shoes, pulled his pants up to my breasts, tied his belt in a knot around my waist, and hit the boards. We didn't do much more than improvise around the *shim sham*, but Gregory Hines broke the spell that had been put on women tap dancers, and as if we were the sleeping beauties in the fairy tale, we awoke to his salute — "AND HERE ARE THE WOMEN."

The next year we, the women, were fully integrated into the festival. It was then that Marda and dance critic Sally Sommer initiated the idea of an International Tap Association that would present a newsletter four times a year to inform fans of tap dance where they could see a tap show, take classes, or read about their favorite dancer. This magazine would also publish articles by tap aficionados talking about ideas and illuminating the philosophies of our form. Most importantly, this organization would unite and excite rhythm tap dancers from around the world. All of us at that first festival became founders of the International Tap Association, which is still a literary guiding force for the community.

To the credit of both Marda and Sali, the Colorado Tap Dance Festivals were always great successes. The yearly Portland festival, produced by Jan Corbett, soon followed their model, as did the Boston festival, produced by Jeremy Aliger of the Dance Umbrella. Other festivals came and went, and even in 2003 more were still signing on. These early festivals presented living histories of virtuosity, with the older tap masters and younger artists discovering new choreographic inventions. All races, all genders, and all ages were represented.

The masters, inspired by the energy and enthusiasm of the students, struggled for the first time to break down their rhythms so that they could be understood. Their stories mesmerized the classes and contributed to our already anecdotal, contradictory, and contentious folklore. We younger teachers attempted to create a syllabus that would help the students in a somewhat organized fashion. Steve

Condos and I were the only teachers in the early years really interested in building a syllabus with rudiments and technique to enable the student to develop speed and clarity.

Marda Kirn, now in full support of the women leading the field, invited Lynn Dally and me to curate the last Colorado Festival in 1992. We created a three-week conservatory that has yet to be equaled, with classes in technique, composition, improvisation, and music for dancers. The students, with the guidance of the teachers, created and performed their own choreography, collaborating with musicians on staff to create arrangements that were played live in performance.

Creating a Lineup

The lineup on stage at festivals from Boston to Texas astounded audiences with the artistry and variety of so many dancers with different styles. These lineups introduced the fine art of tap dance to an audience that did not know what to expect. Those of us fortunate enough to be performing in those festivals at the beginning of the renaissance were bursting with excitement and enthusiasm for the return of our beloved form. A single performance might include eight to ten artists whose different styles became instantly discernable. No one copied anyone else, and it was inconceivable that anyone would have been booked for these concerts if they did not have their own unique material and presentation.

Eddie Brown always opened our shows. Dressed in his white tuxedo and white broad-brimmed hat, he set the tone for the whole show quickly and emphatically. He swung his short, four-chorus dances at a medium tempo, developing his rhythms by accenting and doubling up his heels. He set his tempos with crisp, syncopated *time steps* to which he returned after executing *breaks* with a flourish of very hip and complex patterns.

Eddie was a very small, quiet man who always looked like he possessed a secret. When he sat with us on panels for discussion, he always gave a serious admonition to an unanswerable question: "You better watch out or you'll get a bad letter from Calhoun," he would say, looking down into his lap with a little bow, his hat covering his face in finality. We are still wondering, "Who was Calhoun?"

Honi Coles, who had acquired so much experience as master of ceremonies and artistic director of the Apollo Theater in Harlem, was always given the responsibility of creating the lineup and introducing the acts. He knew each spot on a bill required a specific kind of number. If you were on first, you'd better not go on too long. The first act sets up the whole show. If you were on last you could stretch out because no one was waiting to go on. If the audience got bored, people would just walk out, but if you were as dynamic as you should be, they would stand up and welcome the whole cast back on stage.

What Honi loved about Steve Condos, besides his amazing dancing, was that he could put Steve anywhere in the lineup. Steve could open the show, he could close the show, or he could be somewhere in the middle. No matter where Honi put him in the lineup, unlike some other dancers with more temperament, Steve was always gracious and could fulfill his specific spot on the bill.

Steve, one of the few older white artists recognized by black rhythm tap dancers, was originally from Philadelphia. He and his brothers, Frank and Nick, made their mark doing very fast rhythm and flashy *five tap wings* in Hollywood movies starring Betty Grable. After the Hollywood musical became a genre of the past and his two brothers retired, Steve moved to Florida and kept playing his trumpet and piano while working as the entertainment director for cruise ships. Twenty years later the revival offered Steve, now no longer a slave to the restrictions imposed by movie producers, the opportunity to present his vision in an exclusively musical way. Standing center stage in the crouch of a boxer, never traveling more than two feet in any direction, he developed a cappella improvisations from simple rudiments into ever more complex phrasing. It was as if he were on a journey to find the ultimate rhythm, and when he found it, he stopped short and bowed to the thunderous applause. When interviewed about his approach Steve replied, "I just get into a trance and dance."

Honi liked to place his favorite dancer, Chuck Green, somewhere in the middle of the program. Chuck, a longtime resident of New York City, was a serious "listen." He phrased and delivered like a poet. His dances were endless variations of syncopated triplets with surprising doubletime turns and shifts of weight. He often opened his dances with a whole chorus of stylized vernacular movement without taps, twisting his large frame over a subtle slide or a slow drag of the leg while spreading the fingers of his large hands as if he were a puppeteer playing his feet. When Honi saw Chuck was close to closing, he would yell out for him to do one of his favorite steps and keep him on stage just a bit longer and then a little longer.

Chuck was also the master of the non sequitur. We are still wondering what he meant when he told us to "Watch out for the cargo." Or was it "Watch out for the card-

Coles and Bufalino performing "Chair Dance" at 1980 Bear Mountain festival.

board?" Either way it was an inside joke that no one could understand.

Of course there was never any problem keeping Bunny Briggs on stage. He kept dancing his *riff walks* and quick turns, flipping his head, and whipping his hair. He stopped short to give the audience a chance to applaud in the middle of his solo, and finally, when he brought the whole house to its feet, he would walk over to the microphone and tell them how much he loved them.

For a shift and a change Honi presented the Jazz Tap Ensemble, a new and unique tap and jazz music collaborative working out of Los Angeles. Their choreography was highly arranged and filled the stage with rhythm pictures and flowing bodies. If Jane Goldberg, a protégé of Cookie Cook, was on the bill, she would perform her comedic interpretation and tap parody of Edgar Allen Poe's poem "The Raven."

By the mid-1980s, four generations were appearing on the same festival bill, displaying a mesmerizing variety and virtuosity. By this time the precocious young Savion Glover was astounding us with his potential. He was like a sponge, soaking up everything and everyone he saw and heard.

Jimmy Slyde, originally from Boston, had been living in France for many years and was fresh to American audiences. He returned to amaze us with his *slides* and rhythms. Jimmy danced the whole stage while executing beautiful turns and moves that shaped his patterns. He let his *slides* run out to where they wanted — he didn't stop them, he let them go free and enjoyed what he discovered when he got to the end.

Sarah Petronio, an American who grew up in India and immigrated to France, developed a tap program at the American Center in Paris. Sarah initiated the tap revival in France, performing with her company of students. She presented and performed with Jimmy Slyde, partnering with him in nightclubs and concerts. Sarah was new to the American stage but soon became recognized as one of our groove-masters. She danced close to the band, trading bars while talking to them with her taps. She also kept up a repartee with the audience, speaking to them in French, as if she were still on the Rue de la Paix.

Dianne Walker from Boston, with her delicate sound and smooth, close-to-the-floor delivery, was the new kid on the block. A protégée, of Leon Collins, she charmed the audience with a seemingly naive presentation, opening her act with an aside to the band, "Well let's see now, what should we do?"

I often opened the second half of the show. Or, because I was versatile and danced to slow waltzes or sensuous bossa novas as well as fast bebop tunes, Honi could put me where he needed a change, and I'd dance whatever he asked.

Gregory Hines, already a movie star focusing a spotlight on tap dance in *White Nights* with Mikhail Baryshnikov, was often presented in the closing star spot. It was a joy to stand backstage and watch him search for and create new rhythms every eight bars. He improvised his way into a brand new style right there in performance. Gregory created physical forms with African dance movements that propelled his footwork and lent a powerful visual dynamic. He developed a casual delivery, talking to the audience when he had completed a pattern. He took a drink of water from the bottle he brought on stage and began again. From years in show business with his father and brother in the act Hines, Hines and Dad and his success on Broadway in *Eubie*, he brought a confidence, charisma, and fresh approach that could really close the show on a high note. Gregory developed this style of spontaneous composition on the concert stage and transferred it to film in his movie *Tap*. He called his style of choreographic invention "improvography."

The Nicholas Brothers joined us for the first time at the Boston Festival. The brothers, Harold and Fayard, in contrast to many of the improvisational acts on the bill, were slick and polished. They were the acknowledged stars and elder statesmen of our tribe and would close the show, singing and dancing in front of clips from their movie-musical productions.

If Gregory or the Nicholas Brothers weren't on the bill, Honi would often close the show. By the end of the night he had already won the hearts of the audience with his master of ceremonies jokes and intimate, almost confidential delivery. The audience was eager to see him dance. He opened with his tribute to Bill Robinson and then said, "That was Uncle Bo; now this is me." He finished his set with a whir of complicated, subtle, almost delicately nuanced phrases and exited the stage with his long legs pushing *slides* into the wings. Even though he couldn't dance after his stroke in 1987, Honi continued on as our master of ceremonies. His presence, even without taps, meant that every performance would have a high standard of artistic integrity.

Filled with emotion while dancing the final *shim sham shimmy* with all of these incredible performers, I knew these were the glory days, when the stars shown brightly and four generations of the tap dynasty shared the stage with warmth and love for each other. The audiences packed the houses, most of them seeing rhythm tap for the first time. At the end of the concert, jumping up from their seats in a standing ovation, they were sure they could do a *time step* if we asked them to come up on stage, and we often did.

TWELVE

~

Creating the American Tap Dance Orchestra

VIRTUOSO TAP DANCE HAS ALWAYS BEEN the province of the soloist. Even the great duos, trios, or quartets presented only a few choruses of material together before each dancer went into a solo. Everyone appreciates the brilliant solos of Fred Astaire, Bill Robinson, or Eleanor Powell in the movies but no one remembers any virtuosity in Busby Berkley's female chorus lines that repeated a simple *time step* in many directions, traveling down many staircases, in very short costumes. The idea of tap as a solo art is also perpetuated by the image of male dancers competing on street corners or trying to outdo each other when trading eight bars on stage. The personality of the tap dancer often carried the material, suggesting to audiences that it was just an inspiration of the moment, making it seem that anyone can tap dance if they have cleats on their shoes. Tap dancers by nature are individualists wanting to be the best, the biggest, the fastest, or the funniest. So it is not surprising that there have been so few tap ensembles. The whole idea of complex choreography for more than four dancers was unheard of before the tap renaissance.

In 1978 I had a vision of a Tap Dance Orchestra, an ensemble dressed in black ties and tails, placed on the stage like a symphony ... only dancing, their taps creating tones and textures, counterpoints and fugues. I heard arrangements of taps divided into horn sections and rhythm sections. It took three companies and ten years before that visualization finally actualized in the American Tap Dance Orchestra.

It was necessary to train all the dancers for my companies and to replace the women's high heeled shoes with sturdy, flat men's oxfords in order to distinguish the treble sound of the toe tap from the bass sound of the heel. Ensemble tap choreography had always been precision dancing. Everyone danced in a line, executing the same pattern. In contrast, each dancer in the ATDO was required to articulate exact tones and dynamics as well as complex, clear, and precise rhythms. They had to be soloists who could execute their parts of the score and improvise in the open cadenzas.

By 1986 I had been teaching at Fazil's for four years. Fazil's used to be Jerry Leroy's Rehearsal Studio and before that it was Michael's Studio. (In the movie *Easter Parade* Fred Astaire says to Judy Garland, "Let's go to Michael's and rehearse.") The atmosphere at Fazil's was exhilarating. There were four floors of studios with percussive dancers in each room: flamenco dancers, Middle Eastern dancers, and tap dancers, all kinds of tap dancers. Kathy Harris, the receptionist, had been a vaudevillian and the Old Gold tap-dancing cigarette girl on the Ted Mack Amateur Hour. She practiced to the tune "Once In Love With Amy" in A2, the small room with the dirtiest windows facing 8th Avenue. The Copasetics practiced their closing routine to the "Bugle Blues" in A1, the largest room. All the dancers loved A1 because of the beautiful hardwood floors, but they had to dodge the falling ceiling panels caused by the flamenco dancers' heavy footwork overhead in B1. The flamenco dancers' heavy footwork did the most damage to the ceilings and floors of Fazil's. I taught my classes to the music of Count Basie and often rehearsed to the music of Charles Mingus in A4, the quiet room in the back by the fire escape, where Kathy Harris's calico cat sat on the steel steps waiting for her lunch.

I had long since come down off the mountain and was an everyday New Yorker. Dancing, dancing, dancing, sweating, dreaming of new concepts, and finally being able to actualize some old ones. My classes were full, and I had been teaching for long enough to develop dancers from beginner to professional level. Some of them were brilliant. When Barbara Duffy, Margaret Morrison, Russell Halley, Neil Applebaum, Lynne Jassum, and Tony Waag had no difficulty executing the complex rhythms, holding the time and swinging to a very difficult bebop dance that I had composed, I knew it was time.

With the insistent prodding of my student Tony Waag, an ardent supporter of my work, and the encouragement of Honi Coles, who felt it was essential that my choreographed work be created, performed, and handed down to future generations, I assembled the American Tap Dance Orchestra. The dream I had on the mountain of an orchestra of taps playing melodies, arrangements, and counterrhythms with their feet was finally coming to fruition.

I choreographed compositions that could be performed with five dancers as the Chamber Orchestra and conducted forty-five dancers performing on the steps of the New York Public Library for the "River to River Festival." Our touring company consisted of eight dancers, two vocalists, a piano player, a bass player, and myself. I usually played my concertina or brushes with the band and took a solo or two. I was much too interested in what my dancers sounded like and looked like to dance with them. I liked to watch; it was thrilling.

Our first booking was the July 4th Statue of Liberty Festival at Battery Park. For a solid week we performed in the hot sun for thousands. Cookie Cook, Buster Brown, and Tina Pratt were featured artists, and I arranged compositions around them.

Performing my material outdoors was the perfect trial by fire. If those audiences would sit still for us, with all the distractions of sirens blaring and other bands playing, we were on the right track. I didn't adapt my compositions for short attention spans; that would not prove anything. But I did consider the lineup very carefully.

We opened the performance with "Strike Up the Band," especially for the occasion. Eventually we changed the music for this opening to "Take The A Train." It was only a two-chorus dance.

I've always felt that the first number should be brief. And I still find that a short dance is the most difficult to choreograph.

The band played a fanfare in double time for the first eight bars of "Strike up the Band" while the dancers traveled across the floor like thunder and lightening. Then as a unit they moved across the stage in a decrescendo with short, close footwork patterns, loudly accenting every fourth beat. Finally the taps softened to a whisper before they built again to a rousing crescendo. When the tune came in, the groove changed into a mellow swing for a two-chorus dance with only a short and simple counterpoint.

Included in that concert was a medley, opening with "In The Mood," followed by "In a Mellow Tone," and "Just Friends," moving to an a capella section, and then closing with "In the Mood" again. Mimi Moyers and Pat Tortorici were the vocalists for this medley. I like to use vocalists instead of horns for harmony. The lyric they sing gives me a story to tell.

Piano, bass, and drums shared the stage with us. I didn't have a musical director because I love creating the arrangements myself. It's one of the most challenging and enjoyable parts of the choreographic process. I have never forgotten the lessons learned from Sandi Sandiford, the arranger I worked with when I studied at Stanley Brown's studio as a teenager. There are so many details to consider besides the choice of a tune, including the key in which the composition is played. There is a joking reply dancers like to give to the musician who asks what key they'd like to have their music played in — "Oh, I can dance in any key." That is true, but the major or minor key affects the harmonies, and the harmonies affect the emotions of both the audience and the performer. I have been to a few tap concerts where all the songs were played in a minor key, and the audience didn't leave feeling as upbeat as usual. If all the songs are played in a major key, the music is monotonous and offers little emotional range. I like to use all the musical colors, harmonies, grooves, and cacophonies.

"The All Blues ... Tacit ... Latin"

I took a big leap of faith in the audience at the 4th of July Festival, presenting a long and subtle a cappella section in the middle of an "All Blues"/"Blue Bossa" medley. But I needed to know how audiences would respond to compositional tap dance when they hadn't even seen a *time step* for twenty years.

The risk paid off. Even with all the distractions of sirens, ambulances, and firecrackers, the audience was stilled by the subtle phrasing and concentrated delivery of the dancers. This dance also offered me the opportunity of building the orchestral conceit by conducting the opening. Standing in front with arms raised, I introduced each dancer separately with a different rhythm. The fugue built slowly, preparing the audience for the multitude of textures that were to follow. After the fugue, the dance segued into the slow and lyrical "All Blues." The greatest risk was the length of the long a cappella section that followed, with shading, crescendos, and decrescendos, abruptly followed by claps going into "Blue Bossa," building to a three-rhythm counterpoint with very physical as well as rhythmical patterns, utilizing the entire stage. The piece climaxed in a straight line for a repetitive syncopated abrupt ending.

This dance kept evolving. When pianist Darrell Grant joined us, we eliminated "Blue Bossa" and collaborated on an original score that explicitly described the foot patterns. The dance became formally know as *The All Blues ... Tacit ... Latin.*

~

THIRTEEN

The Benefit

Does anyone ever get it right? Raising money is certainly the most difficult part of building and keeping a dance company. Producing a benefit to raise money is always hazardous, and for our first time out the American Tap Dance Orchestra decided to "go whole hog and pay the postage."

Honi donated the first five hundred dollars for the Orchestra's costumes of white ties and tails. Fortunately, I had moved out of my wet basement studio apartment up to the fourth floor on Thompson Street. The ATDO had our first board meeting huddled together in the living room of my tiny new triplex.

I was pleased that Avra Petrides agreed to be on our benefit committee. Avra, a talented actress, producer, and creator of the Bridge Festival in the South of France, had presented Honi, the Copasetics, and me, along with Alan Jay Lerner, Virgil Thompson, and other great talents, to the French country audience. Her production was such an amazing and magical success that I knew she would have much to offer.

Tony Waag, now a featured dancer in the company, also took on the administration of our fledgling company. He was working as a waiter/bartender at Café de Bruxelles on Greenwich Avenue, talking up our project to everyone who came in for French fries with mayonnaise and a glass of wine after work. He brought along Maggie Brown from the Association for a Better New York (ABNY), Randi Glickburg, one of the owners of Fairways, and Justine Pearlman, who soon after the benefit brought us our pro bono lawyer, Willem Remmelink. Cynthia Kirk agreed to work as a pro bono publicist until we got on our feet. George Andrews, Tony's partner at the time, was one of our most enthusiastic members and loved to scheme, party, and pass around the cocktails.

At board meetings, because there was so little space, I always sat on the fourth step of my spiral staircase overlooking the living room. That way when I got nauseous from all the considerations of bylaws, applications for nonprofit status, and the excitement everyone was expressing while planning this huge event, I could climb up the four more steps to my bed and lie down until my stomach settled. Building a company with the size and vision of the Orchestra was like being pregnant and giving birth. The more everyone else wanted it, the less I did. I couldn't stand asking anyone for money and hated going to parties, much less planning one.

And I couldn't believe, when Honi suggested doing the benefit at the Cotton Club in Harlem, that everyone else jumped all over the idea.

"My God," I said. "How will anyone get there? That journey is rough, it's under the elevated subway way up on 125th Street."

George chimed in, "We'll hire limos for everyone. We'll drive them to Harlem in limousines. And we'll have Sylvia's cater the soul food."

"I know the owner of the Cotton Club," Honi said. "I helped him put the place together. He'll give us a deal. Believe me, it's spectacular. Everyone will want to be there ... I'll get Dick Cavett."

But I knew we would need a great deal of money simply to prepare for the benefit. Lots of money, in the thousands. So cocktail parties began, and all the dancers dressed up in their one good outfit and sat around with crossed legs looking very important, talking tap to prospective funders, daughters and sons of funders, and distant cousins of friends of funders. Videotapes of our performances and my choreography ran nonstop, hopefully exciting those people new to tap dance as well as instructing them on what was unique about our offering. I was amazed and caught almost speechless when anyone handed me a check. The whole process was so one-on-one for someone like me who had always been a loner, never asking anyone for anything. Now I had to stand for myself, stand for tap dance, and ask for help. The generosity of our first funders was a life-altering experience.

The publicist said, "We have to have stars. Lots of stars. The newspapers want stars." Fortunately George liked to call stars. "I'll call Gwen," he said.

"Oh, Gwen Verdon loves tap dance," Honi said. "She was a great tap dancer herself; she dubbed the movie tracks for the stars in musicals."

Invitations were made and rejected and made again. Everyone addressed and stamped. Tony called me breathlessly. "Guess what? Rudolph Nureyev was the first person to reply. I got his RSVP today." "Is he coming?" "No, he can't make it, but isn't it great that he RSVP'd?"

Every day the papers said we needed more stars and more. Soon it was not only Gwen but Tommy Tune and Robert Duval who said they could make the benefit. Robert was going out with one of our dancers and agreed to perform the tango with her.

I was busy creating choreography. We would introduce a new work, a piece I was working on that had rhythm patterns I didn't want to identify yet. I was working in a stream-of-consciousness mode, without music, without a time signature. I created long extended phrases against very short traveling patterns. Margaret Morrison cried, "This will never work. It doesn't fit!"

"Why would I give you something that doesn't fit?" I said petulantly, secretly wondering why I thought I knew. I just knew, that's all.

Finally, I began to see that the work was swinging between 6/8 tribal patterns and the blues. One night, sitting on a little folding chair on my three-foot-by-three-foot terrace that overlooked Livorno's Italian restaurant, I listened to a recording of the Charles Mingus band playing his "Haitian Fight Song." "That's it!" I shouted out loud, finally understanding what my counterpoints were saying and where they were heading.

For the first and only time in my life, I sat down and wrote out five lines of rhythms on music paper. I hadn't created a melody yet, so I transferred the melody of "Haitian Fight Song" from the flute to the feet for the opening of the dance. I also discerned a short rhythm, way in the back of his arrangement, like a Scottish motif: *ruuum ruuum ruuum ruuuum*. This motif I used as the connector with at least four dancers holding the pattern in a fighting, rocking motion throughout the dance. It was a most powerful visual – such an elegant and unusual short rhythm to hold all the long rhythms together. The whole piece finished with a rush, musical arrangement and all. It would be done for the benefit, which by now had taken on the proportions of a celebrity event.

So many details ... we were spending so much money, and the stock market was slipping like a greased pig through a rickety fence. Tickets were selling but donations were off.

Then, the week before the event, our benefit chairman, my mentor and my dearest friend, Honi Coles, fell to the ground at the Chicago airport on his way to perform in *My One and Only.* He was sent to the hospital and diagnosed with a stroke, but he insisted on traveling back to New York. He had another stroke on the plane. We visited him in New York at St. Vincent's Hospital. Daily his flowered and carded room was filled with admirers. He was a mysterious character, often aloof and unavailable, but now everyone could find him and everyone did. Portia Marx, one of our supporters in for the benefit from Portland, Oregon, leaned close to him, her cleavage whispering good cheer in his ear. He was a king on the throne of his hospital bed. His speech was slightly slurred, but he acted as if his paralyzed right leg was simply a nuisance that would go away after he rested for a few days.

I continued lining up the acts for the show. Performance artist and physical comedian Bill Irwin agreed to perform, as did Bob Berky, another New Vaudevillian. They were two of the world's greatest clowns, one with a top hat, out of control, tripping and sliding over the stage in slippery tap shoes, and one on a make-believe motorbike, blowing on a kazoo.

The klieg lights were set up outside the Cotton Club, lighting two blocks with regal illumination. Sylvia delivered the soul food: ribs, yams, collard greens, sauerkraut, meatballs, sweet potatoes, etc., etc., etc. George worried that "Son of 'Fes'" (Cab "Fes" Calloway's son) might not show up. He warned us to be extra nice to Liza Minnelli's secretary, who turned out to be Liza's secretary's secretary. He exalted over the appearance of Gloria Steinham with Mort Zucherman, Bobby Short, and David Dinkins — not to mention Dick Cavett and Gwen Verdon and all those good friends, funders, and critics dressed to the nines who accompanied them for the birth of a tap dance company.

As I was about to make an announcement apologizing for the absence of Honi Coles, he and his wife, Marion, drove up in a limousine in front of the Cotton Club. He had escaped from the hospital for this one night, and with the help of Tony and Neil managed to climb the stairs to the second floor balcony where he laughed and bought drinks while presiding over the benefit.

Cookie Cook danced, followed by Jimmy Slyde, who drove all the way from Boston to perform for us. Barbara Duffy fed me droppers of the homeopathic remedy devil's claw, while I tried to get my foot, swollen from gout, into my tap shoe.

The crowd cheered for the American Tap Dance Orchestra. Our company was launched by show business royalty and political luminaries.

At the end of the night as the crowd dispersed, escaping into their limos like woodchucks into their burrows, Barbara, Tony, Margaret, and I cleaned up. Somewhat delirious with exhaustion, I packed up some of Sylvia's delicious sauerkraut and carried it on my lap in the station wagon as we dropped off the company members and Liza Minnelli's secretary's secretary. We hit a bump and the slaw slopped all over my Salvation Army red-fox coat, so we stopped the car, and I put the pan under a tree beside a hydrant for the birds or the dogs.

Honi, meanwhile, returned to the hospital in his limo.

When we did the accounting to see how much money we had made from our benefit for our spring season, we saw that we had spent $23,000 and taken in only $18,000. Honi said, "I guess you already had your spring season this winter at the Cotton Club. But look at it this way: you've got your tuxedos. You're ready to go to work."

FOURTEEN

~

PBS Great Performances

GREGORY HINES ALWAYS KNEW when to give tap dance a boost. He brought attention to tap improvisation and rhythm tap in the movie *White Nights*, created the movie *Tap*, and presented a tap concert at Carnegie Hall that included many of us who had been dancing in the Tap Festivals around the country. His stature brought a much-needed focus to tap dance.

In 1989 the Public Television series *Great Performances* presented "Tap Dance in America with Gregory Hines," a special presenting vintage as well as contemporary tap dancers. A motif had been developed around Sandman Simms, who wanted Gregory to loosen the screws of his taps for a different sound. Gregory of course refused, because he wanted his own sound. The argument allowed a touch of comedy as a running gag throughout the show, which showcased the dancing of Bunny Briggs, Jimmy Slyde, Buster Brown, and The Women! as Gregory introduced them: Dianne Walker, Jenny Lane, and Camden Richmond. Fred Strickler danced a classical piece. Gregory danced duets with himself and a long a cappella solo, as did Savion Glover, then just fifteen and as charming as he was brilliant. One could easily see in this performance how Greg's style was influencing this young prodigy. From Broadway, Greg Burge and Hinton Battle combined acrobatics with their taps, and Heather Cornell's company, Manhattan Tap, performed to a bebop tune, "Scrapple from the Apple."

Since Honi could no longer dance because of the stroke that left his right leg paralyzed, I had the privilege of teaching our version of the very slow *soft shoe* "Taking a Chance on Love" to Gregory and Tommy Tune. In one week's time, I used all my powers of gentle coercion and persuasion to help them blend their two disparate styles into one smooth, articulate and synchronized *soft shoe*, the most difficult *soft shoe* that was ever created. Tommy and Gregory, in white tuxedos, danced their most elegant best, presenting this dance as a tribute to its creator, Honi Coles.

The American Tap Dance Orchestra performed "The Haitian Fight Song." It was a real honor to be included in this production, but I was very disappointed when Gregory told me to cut my dance from seven to three minutes. I couldn't imagine how I could squeeze all the different parts of this work into three minutes. But for a change, I did not contest the decision and allowed myself to take direction. The producers insisted that I use the whole twelve-piece band instead of my usual piano, bass, and voices. It was an arranging challenge. How could I keep this big band from drowning out the taps?

Harold Wheeler was the musical director and arranger. He struggled valiantly trying to get the effect I wanted. In rehearsal with the band, however, I knew immediately it was not going to work. Finally, I asked the horn sections to mute their instruments, and only the trumpet played full without the mute. If Harold had not been such a gentleman I might have lost that gig, because instead of working through him, I spoke to the band directly, and very emphatically. Musicians are not used to taking directions from dancers, but the final arrangement succeeded, and after Gregory and I danced a short introduction together I performed with the company. The dance took off with tremendous power and energy — and most importantly you could hear every tap. As it turned out, "The Haitian Fight Song" benefited from the edits, and I discovered that three minutes of dancing was quite a long time on television and quite enough. Honi sat up front in the audience beaming as Tommy and Gregory danced his *soft shoe*. He almost busted his buttons with pride and relief when our difficult music was perfectly executed by the band, and the audience responded to "The Haitian Fight Song" (which he felt was so obscure) with such enthusiasm,

~

FIFTEEN

A Home for Tap Dance

Sitting at the head of the table at the board meeting, I had to plead my case for finding a space, a home for the American Tap Dance Orchestra.

—We can't get enough time in a big enough space to develop and rehearse new material.

—We are not welcome to tap dance on most dance studio floors, or we are offered rubber or marly floors which have no sound and make our feet swirl around inside shoes that are stuck to the floor, and this makes our knees torque.

—We are treated like pariahs for making too much noise or for leaving aluminum gray marks on pristine highly polished floors that you could eat off of, but not walk or tap dance on.

—We cannot find appropriate venues for performance.

—We have no place to develop programs or teach a comprehensive curriculum, no place to meet and greet, have tap jams, lectures, and workshops.

—Most important, I cannot create a body of work out of a suitcase.

All these were the reasons I gave to the board in pressing the ATDO's urgent need for its own space. They weren't sure. Even as I was scouring neighborhoods for the right environment for my company, the board members were shaking their heads in dismay. Only Willem Remmelink, our lawyer, and Sean Young, a movie actress, student, and tap enthusiast, thought that it was imperative. Tony agreed tentatively, but the others thought it would be too expensive and difficult to find and even more difficult to keep.

One seventy Mercer Street, between Prince and Houston, offered a great location, a walk-in off of the street into what could be our office, greeting space, and a balcony for the long contiguous underground level where classes and performances could be observed from above. There was a problem. It was a raw space: long and narrow like a tunnel, with cement basement floors and no dividing walls. A rickety ladder, looking like a toothless vagrant, was our only way to connect to the lower level; we would need to build a long staircase. As rough and raw as this potential studio was, its vast expanse was elegant and welcoming.

Standing on the street-level landing looking down into the great cavernous space with forty-foot ceilings, I imagined the roar of dinosaurs and sought ancient secrets buried under the rocks that supported the brick wall. I saw that paintings would look glorious on the great wall viewed from afar and above, and I could imagine the acoustic resonance of music and taps resounding through the space. For some reason I didn't worry that the plumbing for the whole building would be buried behind walls we erected. After all, wasn't my father a professional contractor and my mother one of the most sought-after interior decorators in Marblehead, Massachusetts? Hadn't my ex-husband and I rebuilt a church and built a farmhouse with our own hands and imagination? Didn't I know how to do this?

Finally Willem and I prevailed and the board agreed. We signed the lease, knowing that it could take between eighty and one hundred thousand dollars to renovate.

Our landlord put some money for the renovation project in escrow, and Sean Young came forth with monetary help to start. I supplied the rest by donating my grant money for choreography, teaching workshops, and touring my one-person show. It was a steady flow, a river running from my pocket into the renovation. Though we beat the bushes from Houston Street to Riverdale, we could find no funders interested in helping a tap company procure or renovate a space. Government agencies, corporations, and individual funders loved donating money to the ballet, but not to America's own indigenous art form, tap dance. Shouldn't we be dancing on street corners?

We couldn't keep paying rent without money coming in, so even though we weren't finished with the renovation, we opened our space with a November workshop. The wood-cut sign carved by Jebah Baum hung proudly from the ceiling as if it were announcing the entrance to Mecca:

WOODPECKERS TAP DANCE CENTER
& INTER ARTS SPACE
HOME OF THE AMERICAN TAP DANCE
ORCHESTRA

Tony and Barbara Duffy prepared to register people under a tent in the makeshift office set up downstairs. Our carpenter, Bob Beswick, dragged his tools, long pine boards, and table saws up the rickety staircase, past incoming dancers with their backpacks or tap shoes hanging from their shoulders. Sawdust filled the air and the varnish on our "state of the tap dance art" maple floors was still drying.

I was so nervous about our first workshop that I went out to the local bar for a straight vodka on the rocks and then paced back and forth on the sidewalk waiting for more students to arrive — hoping more students would arrive, hoping the teachers would arrive, and praying no one would fall through a hole in the floor. And they did come, and when they did Margaret Morrison welcomed them with her usual grace and charm and escorted them safely to their classes. Cookie Cook, Gregory Hines, Buster Brown, and I taught at the first Woodpeckers workshop. Other activities proceeded at a breakneck pace. The space offered ATDO company members a home where they could teach classes and rehearse their own material as well as mine. Dancers from around the world found us quickly. It was as if we had put out birdseed, and the dancers were so hungry for tap food and a wonderful sprung maple floor to peck on that they flew over continents to find us.

Soon after opening Woodpeckers we wanted to present a performance series. We appealed to Bobby Short, who was on our advisory board, for a piano; we couldn't begin without a piano. Bobby didn't find us just any piano; he gave us a brand new Baldwin upright with such a beautiful, powerful sound that we never needed any microphones. With audiences crowding the bleachers, leaning over the balcony, and sitting on each other's laps on the long stair-case, new choreography performances were presented and new talents were discovered.

In this beloved space, I created *The American Landscape*, a complete evening-length work celebrating the music of Hoagy Carmichael. As we began work on "Stardust" and "Skylark" we got a call from Hoagy Carmichael's son, Hoagy Bix, who wanted to come and see what we were up to. So, I wondered, is he going to want royalties in advance? But instead of royalties, Hoagy wanted to be a part of the process. He loved tap dance and was excited that we were creating an epic work to his father's music. He immediately joined our board.

I envisioned *The American Landscape* as a tribute to the mountains, rivers, and creatures of this land. Carmichael's music spoke directly about the landscape in "Old Buttermilk Sky," "Riverboat Shuffle," "Memphis in June," "Baltimore Oriole," "Blue Orchid," and "Georgia," as well as about the gentle people who enjoyed the creatures and the foliage like "Judy" and the very tired person in "Old Rocking Chair's Got Me." Neil Applebaum and I collaborated on a duet for him and Mark Goodman to Carmichael's Second World War song "Billy Dick," and I created a duet for Russell Halley and Andrea Goodman to "Ooo What You Said." Barbara Duffy created her bright up-tempo solo to "Moon Country," and Margaret danced her elegant traveling solo to "How Little We Know." Before she performed her solo, I sat Robin Tribble down at the piano to plunk out "Heart and Soul," a song that every one in my generation played with one finger on the ivories. Olivia Rosenkrantz and Pat Tortorici sang "River Boat Shuffle" and "Jubilee," Tony sang and did a *sand dance* to "Stardust," and I took a swinging chorus of "Sing Me a Swing Song and Let Me Dance." I played my original melody "Swan Song" on the concertina, with my face covered by a generic white mask, while the whole company danced "The Indian" solemnly, with their black tuxedo tails flying like feathered bustles. This piece ended in a circle and transitioned into the joyous Carmichael tune "Riverboat Shuffle," which was also sung by Olivia and Pat while playing

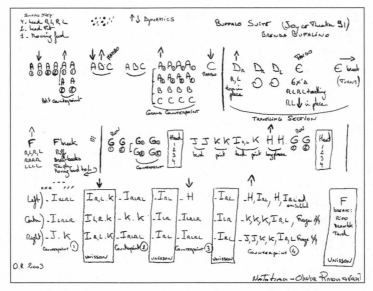

Pictorial notation of the "White Buffalo Dance," created by American Tap Dance Orchestra dancer Olivia Rosenkrantz.

tambourines. To me this transition signified the historical segue from the Native Americans to the white settlers.

The core of my work has always been inspired by the living spirit of nature, and even though I was no longer living next to the Wallkill River, creating *The American Landscape* kept the river living in me.

Having a home at Woodpeckers also offered the time and space to perform the compositions I was creating, as works in progress. Here I created the *White Buffalo Suite* with a cappella contrapuntal rhythms and precise idiosyncratic arm positions and postures for dramatic uniformity. Darrell Grant and I wrote music for the *Flying Turtles,* with melodic, rhythmic, and visual motifs inspired by our indigenous peoples.

Our space was an Inter-Art Space as well as a dance space. Jeb Baum was curator of the revolving art exhibits, many of which were incorporated into theatrical or dance productions. The paintings and sculptures filled the space with color, shape, and depth of experience. The art openings were grand affairs of conversation, dress-up clothes, and white wine with cheese. These events gave the tap dancers and the visual artists an opportunity to meet and greet new audiences.

It took the ATDO board a long time to get used to the name Woodpeckers. They didn't think it was a sophisticated enough title for such a grand establishment with such big ideas. But it seemed to me that no matter how elegant its surroundings, tap dance should always be accompanied by humor and wit wherever it finds itself. When Honi Coles called the studio looking for me, he would always ask for "the Head Pecker." Honi agreed with me that we needed animal and bird totems for good luck, and indeed that's what tap dancers do — peck wood.

Buffalo Suite (photo Jebah Baum)

~

SIXTEEN

The ATDO on Tour

OUR APPEARANCE ON THE PBS SPECIAL "Tap Dance in America" kept the ATDO touring throughout America for three years, including the trip through the Midwest we called "The Tour from Hell." After taking a plane to a central spot, we piled into vans for miles and miles of traveling across the prairie, studying the architectural wonders of A-frame hog houses, finally to arrive in Hayes, Kansas, or Macomb, (pronounced like Mabrush) Illinois. The stage in Macomb was bubbled Plexiglas instead of wood or Masonite. We held each other upright through most of the group numbers and danced in place for the solos.

We were surprised by the welcoming, beautiful, and warmhearted cities like Iowa City, Iowa, where ducks traveled daily from the lake up to and through the local supermarket to where they could safely lay their eggs in their favorite nesting spot. We fell in love with Fayetteville, Arkansas, where tie-dyed shirts still hung from clotheslines, and en-joyed a special sightseeing trip through the Ozarks. We were trapped in snowstorms, missed many hours of sleep, rushed from planes to theaters with no stops in between, endured hours of sound checks, and danced on many very difficult stages. But the company members remained upbeat, and they were kind enough to share their complaints with each other and not with me.

Because many of the ATDO members were talented in life skills as well as tap skills, we were a very happy and compatible group. I appreciated the benefit of having a big company where I wasn't required to "mother" anyone.

The dancers took care of cleaning and transporting their own costumes. Barbara, our dance captain, who had worked in the hotel business, assisted our tour manager with the booking of rooms. Tony, of course, was the administrative director who worked with our agent and handled the money. Margaret and Olivia made sure all of our props were packed in the big trunks, and whichever pianist was playing the tour, Darrell Grant or Frank Kimbrough, carried our music charts.

The dancers paired off on these tours and kept each other company. Hervé Legoff and Olivia were both French and found it a relief to sit together and converse in French. If I was very tired or paranoid, I sometimes imagined they were talking about me and how difficult all this traveling was. But, in fact, they were just making a home away from home for each other, speaking their native language.

Frank Kimbrough shared the contents of care packages sent by his parents, so fresh fruit and candy awaited us at every next hotel in every next mall. It was a very homogenous group and we had a ball, as did our audiences who filled the theaters of two thousand to five thousand seats.

The biggest challenge was the sound check. In our pieces each section of a counterpoint had to be heard clearly in order for the whole rhythmic orchestration to

American Tap Dance Orchestra (bottom to top, left to right):
Margaret Morrison, Barbara Duffy, Olivia Rosenkrantz,
Andrea Goodman, Russell Halley, Neil Applebaum, Brenda Bufalino,
Robin Tribble, Herve Legoff, Tony Waag

blend as one. It was a technical nightmare that needed twelve shotgun microphones, many of which we carried ourselves, as well as our extra speakers, to be placed in the middle of the house at just the right distance from the stage so there would not be a delay.

Between our successful tours and the continual performances at Woodpeckers we had acquired so much of a following that when we secured an engagement at the prestigious Joyce Theater in Manhattan we were sold out three weeks in advance. By this time our repertoire was endless, and because of my excessive nature I wanted to perform everything we ever did, or wanted to do, in this one week.

For this engagement we presented the very contemporary "Touch Turn Return," a work created in collaboration with the composer Carmen Moore. Because of time constraints the creation of this piece was a difficult process. I began creating the dance before Carmen had composed the music. The twenty-minute piece, touching on different musical modes, opened indeterminately, segued into a shuffle rhythm, then into a bright flight in 2/4, into an almost classical Spanish form, finally ending with a fugue where Carmen and I finally caught up with each other in the creative process.

Carmen conducted the dancers and his Sky Music Orchestra from a podium onstage. The drama of the piece lies not only in its musicality but also in the attention the dancers focus on the conductor. They had to sense each other almost telepathically, memorizing and executing patterns that did not link up in any obvious way to the music. There was always the danger of a train wreck. Yet it never happened. The dancers danced as one.

The critics loved this piece, but Honi stood in the wings every night wondering why the audience was so enthusiastic, why they didn't walk out on this avant-garde musical abstraction. To make up for my departure from tradition, I created a special suite dedicated to him that I knew he would love, called *Buff Loves Basie Blues*. Honi loved the Basie band above all others, so I composed and choreographed this suite of *swing* and *soft shoe* dances to music Darrell and I created inspired by the Basie band's arrangements and idiosyncratic musical licks.

The Joyce Theater season was the last time Honi and I performed together on stage. He couldn't dance of course, so we sang his ballads "Get Yourself Another Guy" and "The Doggonest Feelin' Ever" on two stools, and the company dancers danced the pieces we once performed.

The second half of the program was dedicated to *The American Landscape*, which we had been performing as a work in progress for two years. I placed Darrell Grant in the audience at the piano playing the overture, reminiscent of the old silent movie theaters, while original drawings by Jebah Baum depicting totems of our indigenous American culture were projected on a large screen. As the screen lifted, the white buffalos danced forward dressed in white tuxedos and Jeb's large white buffalo masks. The choreographic challenge with the White Buffalo dance was to give the impression of a stampede with only the rhythms, without the dancers traveling very much. It had to be created on an iconic flat plane so the masks could be visually effective. The masks themselves had to dance, every head movement a punctuation. The intermittent nodding of the masks sounded like the snorting of the buffalo and the dancing the pounding of his hoofs.

Honi and I had often spoken about the danger of tap dance surviving only in the personality of solo artists. When the star soloist died or quit tap dancing, tap dance was in danger of being buried once again. We felt that tap dance would only be safe with a substantial repertory that could be carried from generation to generation. Fortunately, in the 1980s through the 1990s there were quite a few companies working and touring: The Jazz Tap Ensemble, directed by Lynn Dally; Rhapsody in Taps, directed by Linda Sol Donnell; Manhattan Tap, directed by Heather

Cornell; and Anita Feldman and Company. Soon to follow were Tapestry, a multiform company directed by Acia Gray, and the youth ensembles Tappers with Attitude, directed by Renee Kriethen and Eyvon Edwards, the North Carolina Youth Tap Ensemble, directed by Gene Medler, and Dynasty, directed by Thelma Goldberg. These companies collected the repertory that many of us created.

There was a time that the ATDO had so much work that I created a second apprentice company, and because of my travels teaching in Europe there were enough dancers who knew my material to create an International Tap Dance Orchestra for intermittent tours in Germany. I also kept performing my solo concerts even though it was physically and emotionally draining to have a touring company and be on tour so much myself. But if I didn't tour with my own show I would loose my stamina, my finesse and speed, and I wouldn't develop any new material for myself.

Woodpeckers was a place for other soloists and companies to rehearse when they came to town, a magnet for new choreographers and young dancers eager to show their *over the tops* at our monthly tap jams. Gregory Hines and the dancers from his Broadway show *Jelly's Last Jam* would burst in after their shows to slam at our jams. Even if you could only do a *time step,* you were welcome, and it was real cheap — as long as you brought your shoes.

The Eastern European Tour

While preparing my music, collecting passports, and packing suitcases for my solo work in Israel, I was preparing the ATDO for a State Department tour of Eastern Europe organized by the United States Information Agency and

Irene Carstone. It was one of the last diplomatic art tours the State Department sponsored. After my tour of Israel, teaching and performing for producer Avi Miller in Tel Aviv and Ranana, I promised to meet the dancers under the clock in Ankara, Turkey. Instead, I was stranded inside a waiting room alone, watching the ATDO trunks pass by the window. I had been on tour for so long that now it seemed I was lost to the world forever. I felt desperate and semihysterical until finally a small man who didn't speak English came and grabbed all my bags. He also dragged me, protesting all the way, to the bus where all the dancers sat happily waiting, and we were on our way to perform throughout Turkey, Cyprus, Poland, Latvia, and Estonia.

Turkey loved our rhythms, and the Turks were the first audience to think our show was too short. At our last performance in Istanbul, Turkish musicians joined us and we danced the *shim sham* to their music. The musical meters weren't aligned, but we ended up together, smiling, hugging, and kissing. The best stage I ever danced on, and the theater with the best acoustics, was a small theater in northern Cyprus. I tried forever to adjust my microphones for the sound check. Finally in desperation I turned off all the microphones, and the acoustics were perfect without any amplification.

Poland was the first ex-Communist country we visited. The people wore a heavy spirit on their shoulders, and all the monuments were voluminous. The bulky form of Chopin brooded in the park while the chamber orchestra played his music, and the audience ate lunch from small paper bags. The architecture, too, seemed to brood as it waited for a brighter day. At that moment democracy didn't seem to offer much comfort or security to the Poles.

In our hotel, the light struggled to shine through crystals in chandeliers made of bottled glass. The people of Poland carried books of their favorite poets under their arms and were eager to recite their own poetry to us. Art was everywhere; it embraced them and lifted their spirits, and their hardships and poverty were forgotten when they watched our tap dance and listened to the bright and optimistic music of Hoagy Carmichael.

The people of Latvia and Estonia were ecstatic. The communist regime had finally imploded without a fight, and they were free — poor but free. In the square outside my window in Riga stood the statue of Melda, the female symbol of freedom. The people of Latvia, who had been barred from her presence during the Russians occupation, were finally free to visit. Inspired, but with my dresser barricading the door against bandits and burglars, I composed the monologue "I Will Return," which also eventually found its way into the libretto of a future tap opera, then not even a dream.

> *I will return and bring it back from both sides now*
> *What has been lost . . . what has been found*
> *I have learned to read the rings of trees*
> *And dance the dance of leaves . . . falling*
> *Standing in the square I follow fumes*
> *Before they reach the air*
> *Breathe fire into dust*
> *Give birth to snapdragons*
> *Weave garlands for the hair*
> *Of sweet perfumes and colors*
> *Lavender and Mustard*
> *Mournful cries haunt the night with harmonies*

Distant from the stars . . . they have traveled here
And must be taught and then returned
To graves long trampled on and long forgot
But I am one to bring it back
From both sides now
What has been lost
What has been found

At a reception after our concert in Estonia, the state dance company of Tallinn worried about how they would support themselves now that the Communist regime no longer guaranteed their dance seasons with steady salaries. I suggested they had to start selling things as American companies did and support themselves by any other means, using their wits and precious creative energy just to survive.

This tour made me very proud to be an artist and to bring the spirit of America through its own indigenous art form, tap dance, to Eastern Europe. We could feel the temperature rise with warm feelings and smiling faces from an audience who only two hours before had entered the theater depressed and impoverished. The USIA organizers were eager, competent, and helpful; I was delighted to know that one of our government agencies ran so efficiently. I was not happy though, when at the last dinner, after the last performance, a new representative of our government who had just arrived in Eastern Europe, informed me that, after our tour, they were not sending any more artists abroad as ambassadors. Now they would be sending businessmen and computer experts. The government thought they would be much more helpful than artists in spreading the values of democracy. Capitalism had a much less ambiguous message than tap dance or poetry.

~

SEVENTEEN

Beginnings & Endings

Summer over
Leaves some of them red or dusty brown
Fallen early . . . early fall
Crystal skies show yellow on the green leaf
Skies blue as a crisp handshake of autumn
Before the solid grip of ice and snow
A time here on the mountain ridge is an inward breath
The lace of tree tops . . . light through the leaves at dusk
Not long the summer and long summer days
I go into the sparkling cellophane air
Some care is left behind me
The dark outline of a shadow always there.

This is an excerpt from the tap opera that I began to write
even before I knew that I was going to create the tap opera.
I knew that there were voices and taps and no more beginnings or endings of routines, but instead a continuous
libretto with one piece flowing into the next. There would
be no more applause in the middle of a dance or even the
end of the dance, no more applause until the end of the

story. And I knew that the story would take its time and would take time to tell.

As I was embarking on this new journey of combining voice and taps with the dancers and jazz singer Jay Clayton, there was a foreshadowing of trouble, a haunting.

The headless horseman came riding into Woodpeckers on the back of an insurance policy, as icy and mundane as only an insurance policy can be, that wanted to charge thousands of dollars to the ATDO for forty-four employees when Tony was our only one. We were the test case for the State Insurance Workers Compensation Fund. That makes a lot of sense: let's go after the arts organizations that can hardly hold their heads above water and test their endurance. Let's push them down and see how long they can stay underwater without breathing. That's what it was like for two years, in and out of court contesting their findings, which looked like chicken scratches when produced on paper as evidence, chicken scratches that only a rooster could read. Even though he could not read the evidence, the judge always found it easier to rule in the insurance fund's favor. Our board lost heart, and Tony and I walked in circles shaking our heads and wringing our hands in despair and confusion.

At the same time Jesse Helms, the senator from North Carolina, also decided to make war on artists and tried to shut down the National Endowment. He didn't succeed entirely, but he did, with the help of congress, succeed in cutting funds so drastically that individual artists like myself could no longer apply for fellowships, the fellowships that had funded new work and rehearsals for the ATDO. The civic centers, symphonies, and small theaters across the country had their budgets cut so deeply that they could present nothing more controversial or less commercial than *Mary Poppins*. Usually the ATDO was booked a year and a half in advance, but now things were slowing down considerably.

And so was Honi Coles. I could see it, feel it, feel his interest in life slipping. I responded to these feelings by writing poems on the passage of time and created a one-person show called *Unaccompanied*. I traveled alone, without musicians, because theaters could no longer afford my band. Woodpeckers was a perfect place to premier *Unaccompanied*. It was all about birds (I closed the show with "Bye, Bye Blackbird"), art, and loss, and included my poem "Who Calls," which also found its way, eventually, into the tap opera.

> *Who calls? Do you have white hair? Do you have teeth?*
> *Up here songs sing themselves like waters running*
> *That snow leaves melting down the red rocks*
> *Like a soft silent female form, weeping*
> *Not ever is she not weeping ... blood of running ice*
> *Who calls or barks or sings?*
> *Do you have black wings? Do you have teeth?*
> *Frog does not live here anymore*
> *Nor brother or sister buffalo calf*
> *Nor tall trees or small trees*
> *Only jack rabbit and coyote are listening ... alone are listening*
> *Who calls? Have you lost your eyes? Have you lost your teeth?*
> *Who calls to the long standing emptiness?*
> *Erect as a soldier without an arrow, without a sword*
> *Who calls? Who Calls? Who calls?* (1992)

I should have known, should have recognized that some dark cloud came into the studio with Honi that Valentine's

Day. Students had been waiting a long time to hear the master talk on tap dance. After his recent stomach operation, Margaret had to coax him to come and speak at our workshop.

She met him at the door. She was the director of this project, so I stood on the sidelines. He was hugging his trench coat close to his body because he was still shivering from the cold, even though the room was very warm. I should have noticed that he leaned too heavily on the banister while lifting his lame leg, impatiently trying to negotiate the stairs. But, he was as usual smart and elegant, dressed in his black and gray tweed jacket, black trousers, and gray turtlneck sweater. He smiled sweetly as people said hello and gained strength from their enthusiasm. Still ... I should have recognized how firmly his jaw was set and how his usually luminous eyes seemed cloudy and dim.

I had been to Oregon on a choreography commission and was miffed he had not consulted me about whether to have the operation. He usually consulted me on almost everything. I guess I didn't notice how thin he was because I was so puffed with myself and my own recent choreographic triumphs. Everything seemed so normal after the lecture when we went to Livorno's, our favorite restaurant, for spaghetti Bolognese and then back to my apartment right across Thompson Street for one of our long talks on the hard straight-backed sofa.

I had to leave the next day for Israel and the Eastern European tour. I called him from Ankara in Turkey to tell him how the audience felt our two-hour concert was too short and laugh with him for always telling me my concerts were too long. I called from Bursa and told him about the ceramic tile I had purchased; called him from Warsaw to tell him Tony was in the hospital with kidney stones. It felt so strange to be calling him; usually it was he who was on tour, and I who was home receiving his calls.

I was standing in front of the hotel at the Colorado Dance Festival when I saw him for the first time in three months. He got out of the limousine wearing a white shirt and black pants buckled so tightly they looked like a skirt. His thin hands shook, parting the air as if it were water. His already thin face was now all bone. When we went to lunch, he didn't eat and hardly spoke, but soon we were arguing as usual over the lineup for the show or over how to do a step. I felt somewhat jealous and isolated as his old partner Cholly Atkins joined him for a lecture, talking to the students as if they were still partners. But it was I who would dance for him, be his legs for him, while he taught his class sitting down, banging his cane on the floor whenever the dancers executed one of his figures incorrectly.

This festival that Lynn Dally and I curated was the most comprehensive festival we had ever had, and I was a little encouraged about Honi's condition as his enthusiasm grew during the three-week conservatory. I even watched him eat a pork chop at the restaurant after the last show. But it was a short-lived reprieve. The next time I saw him was in St. Luke's Hospital back in New York City, when Tony, Barbara, and I brought him a pumpkin for Halloween. He told me then that he was dying. It was all over by November.

And it all seemed over. How could I care about what I created if he was not there to fuss over how I created it, what music I was using, or how long it was? And how could I walk the city streets and not be looking into the Corner Bar to see if he was drinking a Dewars and water, listening to Lance Heyward on the piano.

Immediately, as if responding to a call from a mother whose womb I could crawl back into, I headed for the Shawangunk Mountains, found a cottage that needed to be rebuilt and didn't have too much light. Except for trips on the Adirondack Trailways to New York City for rehearsals at Woodpeckers and meetings to resolve the case with the state insurance fund, I sat and watched woodpeckers, chickadees, and cardinals frantically swirl around the full bird-feeder I hung from a tall white pine. Fortunately for me, I could not afford to cancel any engagements. I had to keep working and responding to new queries. But what I really wanted to do was take the mountain inside of me and climb up the Shawangunks to the western promontory, Gertrude's Nose.

Soon after Honi's death, my mother, Marge, was diagnosed with Alzheimer's. She and Honi had become very good friends over the years. Both my mom and Honi exuded charm, elegance, and beauty that did not diminish as they got older. I often felt like a child sitting and listening to them tell stories of their early years in show business. They both also had a lot to say about my performances and creative process, and when we were all together they liked to agree on my shortcomings and praise my accomplishments. Now the two people in the world I danced and sang my songs for were gone. Even though my mother was alive, she no longer remembered that I was her daughter.

Just before her husband sold all of her dogs, all her precious antiques, and the house she had restored from a wreck, just before she went silent, I visited her in Massachusetts. Of course, in trying to make conversation I would say, well you remember this or that, but she never did, and became perturbed by my efforts to jog her memory. She said petulantly, "Can't we just sing?" So I took her in the car, she loved to be in movement, and we rode the coastline from Swampscott to Beverly, to Gloucester, singing.

We sang together for three hours, every tune she ever knew. Over and over we sang "Somewhere Over The Rainbow," "Always," "Sentimental Journey," "I'll Be Seeing You," "Embraceable You," even "The Donkey Serenade." How was it she couldn't talk but could sing and remember every word to every song? How was it her beautiful soprano voice floated over the melodies when she couldn't even say her grandchildren's names? Three weeks later I returned with my tape recorder so I could record our hours of singing. It was too late; now her hands simply ran over each other restlessly. The only semblance of Marjorie left was the way her graceful fingers played around her eyes and her lips, and how she recognized the beauty of a sunset or remarked at how a tree branch should be trimmed.

I didn't want to dance anymore, but of course I had to. That's how I made my living, but it seemed so futile, like spitting in the wind, until her husband moved her to Florida and the day I went to visit for the first time. Traveling down the escalator at the airport, I saw her standing beside him. He looked like a giant and she like a lost child, hair uncombed, clothes wrinkled with mismatched colors and frayed seams. "That's not my mother," I thought, "who had shoes and hats to coordinate every outfit." Her husband asked her, as he pointed to me, "Do you know who she is?" "Of course," Marge answered, "She's the Girl Who Dances."

How I longed for her to know that I was her daughter, but if "The Girl Who Dances" was how she remembered me, I had to remember her too. Eventually my feet began to remember they were the feet of a dancer and began to act accordingly. And finally, in 1995, my spirit remembered where it caught the wind and that was in the Northwest.

Reggie Bardach liked to produce "Tap on Saturdays" in Seattle. She had presented all of my one-person shows over the years, and now she was game to produce a workshop for Jay Clayton and me to begin collaborating on "The Tap Opera." Jay was a jazz singer with a unique improvisational style; her sound was organic, like bubbles softly floating the notes up through her throat, singing like a bluebird, screeching like an owl or a red-tailed hawk, and popping like firecrackers when they reached the air. She knew the standards, could swing them or croon them, and could teach her unique style of free jazz. She asked me quite simply, "What is a tap opera?" I handed her a book of my poems to choose from and said, "Let's find out."

She worked on original vocal compositions with her singers for the weekend, and I worked on the choreography and earth chants with the dancers. During the week we put it all together and the next weekend we opened "The Tap Opera" at a grunge bar in the OK Hotel. We put the audience on the stage and the dancers and singers on the platforms usually placed for the audience. There, with eight singers and eight dancers, Jay and I performed our first collaboration for three evenings. After that week I continued writing the libretto, and wherever I taught a tap workshop I would incorporate my new poems and vocal chants into the tap choreography that I taught the dancers.

In 1996, for the American Tap Dance Orchestra's tenth anniversary, we performed *Gertrude's Nose, a Tap Opera* at Dance Theatre Workshop in New York and again in 1997 in Fürth, Germany, with the International Tap Dance

Members of the American Tap Dance Orchestra in the tap opera Gertrude's Nose. *From left: Brenda Bufalino, Margaret Morrison, Olivia Rosenkrantz, and Sherry Eyster (photo by Carolina Kroon).*

Orchestra at the magnificent Staat Theatre. It was about warriors for the land, about the arduous and treacherous journey trying to save the mountain by dancing and singing toward the final destination, the far west promontory, Gertrude's Nose.

> *Sun comes up red*
> *Broadcasts on the blue and white snow*
> *Still*
> *Still mountain ridge appears again at omphalos*
> *Gertrude's Nose points west*
> *She is by herself*
> *She waits*
> *Streamlined attention of her aquiline presence*
> *Gertrude's Nose the final point*
> *The long-sought destination*

Children climb this mother's lap
Scramble her rocks
Hang from her cliffs
Like marsupials from the breast
Under ice now
Still from frozen snow
Still
Mountain ridge appears again at omphalos
Snow is her fur
Warms her throat
Accentuates her crystalline profile
Gertrude sings
We dance on her thighs
Hang upside down from her granite shoulders
Our hands upon the ground
That's how safe we feel
Confident
She fills the holes of our deep despair
Gives courage to the air
That she will last in it
Not disappear
Gertrude's Nose points west
She is by herself . . . she waits

EIGHTEEN

~

A New Era... New Styles

THE MID 1990S USHERED IN a new era. Honi did not live long enough to see Savion Glover's all-male, hard-hitting show *Bring in da Noise, Bring in da Funk*. Had he been sitting in the front row he would have been so excited to see the dynamic dancing and choreography created by this young man that we had all nurtured backstage at dance festivals and concerts throughout his teenage years. Honi would have been furious, however, at the ridicule Bill "Bojangles" Robinson, The Nicholas Brothers, and other great innovative black artists suffered when *Bring in da Noise* presented them as Uncle Toms who were selling out to the white movie establishment.

Savion's show was a big success on Broadway, and at the same time River Dance, the Irish step dancing company choreographed by Michael Flatly, was taking the country by storm. Both shows were highly produced and highly publicized, appealing to the African American and Irish communities as well as the popular culture. Savion, now dancing to a funk groove, tapped into the music the young hip-hop crowd was listening to. And Irish step dancing, once confined to competitions, was now being presented as a performance art in a show that celebrated the development of percussive dance in Ireland and America, and the blending of African and Irish cultures.

These shows were followed by *Tap Dogs* from Australia, another all-male cast of hard-hitters. Everyone was hitting hard, and River Dance, even recorded the taps to increase their volume, with the dancers dancing in sync to the recorded taps against loud synthesizer music.

Herbin Van Cayseel, alias Sweet Pea, alias Tamango, alias Urban Tap, began to tour his eclectic African-inspired show, often including the dynamic Afro-Cuban tap dancer Max Pollak — again, loud hard-hitters in a highly produced format.

Woodpeckers closed, but Jimmy Slyde was still dancing smooth syncopations and slides with tonality, trying to keep the intimate scene alive at a club called LaCavé in New York. Here Roxanne Butterfly learned to compete and improvise, producing a fierce electricity with her fast fluid taps, and Van Porter, who learned some of Jimmy's style, incorporated it into his own and included some show business jive while dancing his syncopated combinations.

By 1998 the concert field for tap dance as well as for all other forms of dance was open to just a few. Most theaters, now with their budgets shrinking, could present only highly publicized companies or companies with stars like Savion or Gregory Hines that would present no risk. They could also afford to hire the youth companies, because the salaries for nonprofessional companies were lower than for the established ensembles.

Luckily for me I kept my solo career active and could continue performing in my one-person shows or as a guest

artist at jazz and dance festivals. Jay Clayton and I continued our collaboration, creating environments using elec-
tronics and digital delays for vocals, poetry, and dance
fusions called *Tone, Text & Tap.*

I also began collaborating with Joe Fonda, a bass player
who performed with the ATDO for many years and also
played for many of my solo concerts. As a member of his
band for the CD and performance project *From the Source,* I
read from his charts and danced out the rhythms behind a
music stand. Joe also joined me in the band of vibes, guitar,
bass, concertina, vocals, and taps that I created for my CD
"Dancing My Dance ... in another person's dream." With
this band I performed original tunes and sang and danced
to the standards that I loved. Once again, reminiscent of
my avant garde days in the 1970's and the recent collaborations with Jay, I put my taps through an electronic delay. I
missed creating counterpoint with my company, but now
all alone, practicing under the moonlight in my studio, I
overlaid my patterns with an intensity that kept me hypno-
tized for hours.

2001 Tap City

Woodpeckers had been closed for only six years but it felt
like a lifetime to tap dancers struggling in a homeless New
York limbo. For the year 2001, Tony Waag, who we all
thought had given up administrating and ministering to
the tap world, decided to produce an International Tap
Festival on 42nd Street at the Doris Duke Theater. The
cochairmen for the festival were Hoagy Carmichael and
Gregory Hines. Gregory was ecstatic that an international
festival would be back home where it belonged, in New

York City. Tony produced an entire week of classes and performances that brought the whole tap community from America, Japan, Israel, France, Estonia, Brazil, Russia, and Germany to New York. Included in that first week's performances was an evening of "Masters and Mentors," a celebration in memory of the masters, many who had died and a few who were still dancing. These artists had generously contributed to the development of the contemporary dancers, now stylists in their own right, who would honor them by dancing their dances on the Doris Duke Theater stage. Charles "Cookie" Cook was remembered by fifteen dancers dancing his choreography to "Breezin'." Buster Brown watched from the sidelines as twelve of the countries' most renowned dancers danced the last piece he choreographed to "Laura." Deborah Mitchell, director of the New Jersey Tap Ensemble, spoke at length about her mentor Bubba Gaines, I reminisced about my mentor Honi Coles, and Tony and I danced his choreography to "Taking a Chance on Love." The American Tap Dance Orchestra re-formed and danced a suite of my a cappella contrapuntal rhythms entitled "Buff's Greatest Hits."

For this evening of tributes there wasn't a dry eye in the house. The festival not only celebrated the past but also refreshed the tap pallet with outrageous performances and new choreography, such as Josh Hilberman's presentation of an almost nude Tap Warrior. This piece so incensed Savion and Yvette Glover, who were in the audience, that they yelled, "That's not choreography." Josh, who was not only outrageously undressed, but tapping exquisitely, continued his act with aplomb, even as Savion threw insults.

At Tap City new acts were discovered and older artists revered. Tony gave Lynn Dally, Sarah Petronio, and me an entire evening. We presented a show entitled "Tap Divas: Three Pioneers." I wrote a semiautobiographical script with the help of Lynn, Sarah, and Avra Petrides, our director. Dressed in aviator goggles, helmets, and leather jackets, we paralleled the lives of female tap dancers with those of the first female pilots and used quotes from the papers of their early achievements and embarrassments at the hands of a skeptical press.

Russia: A Warm Tap Welcome after the Cold War

Victor and Oleg, producers from Russia, were at the first Tap City festival. By the spring of 2002 they had booked twelve of us on a tour that would have performances in Moscow and Saint Petersburg.

Tap dance in Russia? The Russia before Communism is the Russia I knew, through the novels and plays of Dostoyevsky, Pushkin, Chekhov, and Tolstoy. These writers never mentioned tap dance.

What would Russia be like in the spring? Would it still be cold, would lilacs be blooming in Saint Petersburg? What were the expectations of students, their level of experience? What were the floors like? Would there be tap microphones? Could we conduct classes in English?

Tap dance, like jazz music, has spread its rhythms across continents. If rhythms could make peace, then tap dancers should be the ambassadors. Twelve of us from many parts of America, France and Germany traveled to Moscow to teach and perform for the "Tap Parade." From New York it was Tony Waag, Yvette and Savion Glover, Pat Cannon, myself, and our pianist, Larry Ham. From Los Angeles it was Dexter Jones and Jason Samuels Smith.

Shoehorn, who played the saxophone and tap danced at the same time, joined us from Portland, Oregon. Olivia Rosenkrantz and Mari Fujibayashi were rehearsing at Olivia's family home in France and boarded the plane for Moscow with Sarah Petronio in Paris. Kurt Albert and Klaus Bleis (Tap & Tray) flew into Moscow from Nuremberg, Germany.

Certainly this was a cast disparate enough to create havoc. But only a little chaos ensued. Dexter's luggage came two days late, and Jason Samuels Smith missed the plane and came a day late.

It was a long flight, so when Victor, one of our producers, brought us to the very upscale Metropol Hotel next to Red Square, we were all very grateful. All of us somehow expected the worst. Everybody headed for Red Square right away, except for me. I went to bed.

In the evening it was interviews and dinner, with a little tap jam, accompanied by a not-half-bad Russian jazz trio, in a cozy cellar restaurant. The vodka was better than the prix fixe dinner. I didn't drink any wine the whole time I was there, only vodka — fresh and pure.

Russian tap dancers who would join us for performance and be in our classes joined us for the dinner, now more like a banquet. Vladimir, one of Russia's premier tappers, was there with his two partners, who had hosted Tony Waag and Jerry Ames in years past. Oleg, Victor's partner, who had also been partly responsible for the past visit of Pat Cannon and Dexter Jones, scurried around trying to squirrel up our advance money. Alexander, the tallest man at the table, was a Russian-born actor-dancer, with his own dance company, living in Estonia. We had met him previously on our tour for the State Department. It was the first

time I met Oleko, who would become my favorite Russian
artist, dancing a four-legged tap dance under a large black
raincoat, wearing sun glasses and a checkered hat. The
twins from Czechoslovakia, whose performance in our
concerts included dancing with umbrellas and cigars, sat
quietly and respectfully at the end of the long table. The
last to join us at the table was a long-legged man, who
danced with his little son, and three tap-dancing clowns
from the Moscow Circus. There were probably more acts
to come because the "Tap Parade" in performance seemed
as if it were four blocks long.

Larry Ham, our piano player who had to rehearse all
the acts that used live music, had the disposition of a saint
and was grateful for the skill of the Russian bass player and
drummer who joined us. The Americans and Europeans all
used live music, but most of the Russians, with the exception of Alexander, used taped music. Their musical choices
were old and unusual Tin Pan Alley songs that made their
acts seem surreal and fascinating, as if pulled out of an old
black-and-white film clip. They danced short conceptual
pieces, and were like circus or pre–Second World War cabaret acts. Tap & Tray, from Germany, also had that old
feeling, but their work was classic and hip. Even though
they were spinning trays in their novelty act, their footwork, rhythms, and live accompaniment made their work
feel very contemporary.

In contrast, Olivia and Mari's piece, "Sensimaya," was
extremely modern, performed to an original composition
and danced to taped orchestral music. They dressed all in
black, with their hair slicked back and painted third eyes on
their foreheads, and the dance was intoxicatingly dramatic.
The insistent counter rhythms, arched body postures, tight

physical focus, and rapt attention were startling – a dance of warriors.

Of course there were floor issues – there always are. The floor microphones, which were underneath a painted composition board, were exploding like firecrackers in hot spots and completely dead in other sections. This was fine for dancers like Savion and Jason who liked to dance loud and didn't care about tone and texture or about moving through space more than a foot in either direction. But those of us who wanted to travel or produce subtle tones had to confront the tech people with our truncated English, hoping our instructions would be understandable to a Russian soundman. Hands were thrown in the air, fists clenched, brows furrowed, but finally, by the second of our five performances, we had a pretty decent sound. Sarah Petronio could be heard clearly as she traveled back and forth to the band, making us understand why the word *dancing* follows the word *tap*. Sarah, playful and musical, engaged the band and conducted them through complex improvisations, subtly changing grooves and modes. She pulled the drummer up front with her for a duet with sticks and taps, driving the music with her impeccable swingingness.

Tony Waag – now there's a classic song-and-dance man. He sang and danced to "Just In Time" with a tasty tacitness of riffs and legomania up in front, his elegant showmanship highlighting and giving grace to his eccentric comedic moves. The public obviously remembered Tony from his last visit, remembered his dance jokes, anticipated his antics with glee.

They also joyously remembered Pat Cannon, clog dancer and director of Foot and Fiddle Dance Company, who brought them back to the roots of the form — "a hoot and a holler" filled with audience hand clapping and leg slapping. Dexter Jones, who opened our show every night with a sophisticated and stylish Broadway-style *soft shoe*, joined her for some high kicking and spontaneous stomping which set the audience on fire.

Of course, as in every large group, every type is accounted for while we congregate in the lobby of the hotel. The late types are easygoing, surprised to see everyone waiting. The early types try not to smile sanctimoniously, sucking their teeth while they wait for the late arrivals. There are the ones that forget and loose things, the ones that find the lost things, and those that get stomach sickness but always manage to perform anyway. Our beautiful interpreters were always harried from herding the unruly cattle of stampeding "Shuffle of the Buffalos." And the producers always look worried, never have the money on time, and only smile late at night when the show is over and everyone is safely ensconced at a late-night restaurant eating blinis.

Yvette Glover warmed the hearts of the audience every night with her deep resounding gospel voice, singing "Somewhere Over the Rainbow" as if it were a hymn of supplication to the heavens. Our interpreters quickly became her daughters.

Shoehorn practiced his saxophone backstage, running riffs with his fingers to warm his feet. He was the bridge between the Russians and the Americans, a street performer with high aspirations and tap devotion.

Then, of course, the young ones, Jason and Savion, offered their mind-boggling speed and rhythms. Jason's interpretation of the "Jitterbug Waltz" was musical as well

as driving. Such an old tune for such a young man — a tick-
lish surprise. Savion opened a cappella as usual and segued
into an improvisation on "Oh Nostrovia," dancing until he
turned himself inside out, dancing as if he were barreling
down the Grand Canyon in a paper bag. As their improvisations found their own undetermined course, these dancers stayed on stage and kept dancing until they were ready
to drop. Finding rhythms, building, finishing, and then
searching again as if there had not been twenty acts before
them and as if I didn't have to follow and close the show.

If I could have arrived a half-hour before my number I
probably would have been less agitated. If I didn't have to
follow Savion's forty-minute set, I'd have been less per-
plexed about how I should proceed. This was a new one for
me. Usually I am on right before him, setting up his act the
best I can. Following him and twenty other acts that have
already exhausted the ears of the audience was another
matter.

One night I did my Mingus medley, "Pithecanthropus
Erectus," "Reincarnation of a Love Bird," and "Cell Block
F," building slowly, walking out the floor until I cooled it
down. But the next night in an even bigger hall, I opened
with a vocal of "Blackbird" and closed with a bebop dance
to Louie Bellson's "Interface." For the last show in Moscow I sang and danced my waltz to a "Child is Born" and
finished with the Mingus medley. Fortunately, I have a lot
of material to experiment with, but by the last Moscow
show I begged an earlier placement and happily watched
the rest of the show from the audience.

Moscow was becoming yet another incarnation of itself.
The contrast between the grandeur of the palatial architecture, the royal legacy and tyranny of the Czars, and the

bland, grim architectural stoicism created by the Soviet tyranny was a study in political and esthetic values. How shockingly wonderful it was for us to witness the beauty of the palaces! We were awestruck inside St. Basil's Cathedral and the Kremlin, surprised by the color, the intellectual rigor and dimension of the architectural and spiritual concepts. The rekindling of religious fervor, of passions subdued during Communism, made it even more confusing to try and understand the temperament that succumbed to Stalin while secretly studying tap dance.

Back home everyone is surprised when I remark how good the Russian tap students were. They came from as far away as Siberia for classes. It is not surprising really. Russian dancing has been incorporated into tap dance since Ida Forsyne went there from America in the early 1900s. Incorporated into an American tap routine, steps from their folk dances have always provided flash endings and visual excitement with flips, kosotskys, and acrobatics. Vaudeville artists toured extensively in Ida Forsyne's day, influencing each other, creating this beautiful hybrid form of dance.

During the Soviet era, when jazz and tap dance were banned in Russia, if tap dancers met in the street they had secret codes, asking "Are you 'In The Mood'?" If the answer was yes, then came the announcement that a class was being set up at "Pennsylvania 65000." It was no wonder that all those tap students appreciated each *flap* and *shuffle* as if every new *time step* was delivered directly through us from Tap Heaven, accompanied by Glenn Miller or Duke Ellington.

My favorite memory is probably the overnight train ride from Moscow to St. Petersburg sharing my compartment with Sarah Petronio, who told me some fascinating details about her childhood in India. There is never enough time to sit quietly and talk with beloved peers before the gig is up and we are saying goodbye at the airport, promising to spend more time talking and laughing at the next festival that brings us together again.

~

NINETEEN

Germany, Italy, & Home'
away from Home'

EVEN BEFORE CREATING the American Tap Dance Orchestra in 1986, I began my travels to Germany that continue to this day. For a long time it was students and audiences in Europe that kept the bread on my table and my spirits from sagging. They welcomed me and appreciated my work, even when I performed extended a cappella compositions and long monologues in English, making no concessions to their difficulty in understanding my language. They always seemed to understand, to laugh at my jokes and comprehend my difficult tap phrasing.

On one of my first trips to Cologne an audience member came up to me after the show and announced, "You dance just like Lenny Tristano" (a bebop piano player whom I loved in the 1950s). Then he brought me a tape of Tristano playing and described the similarities in our phrasing and accents. In America the general public didn't know much about jazz, less about Lenny Tristano, and even less about tap dance. The European audience loved jazz. It had not been replaced by rock music or become passé; it was heard constantly in restaurants and on the radio. Musicians everywhere were playing jazz, and I played with many of them. Everywhere I performed it was with a new pickup band. Sometimes the rehearsals were hours long as I tried to explain that the music needed a kick and then tried to explain what a kick was and how to get a kick that would push the music and give it life. Often it seemed that in Europe in the 1980s all jazz was played in minor keys. While I was in Amsterdam teaching my very promising young student and performer Peter Kuit, he took me to a jazz festival called "The Boulevard of Broken Dreams." The music was so sad, and the blues so blue that it took me two days to recover and smile again. But what I loved most was the sincerity, the respect that I was given personally and the respect and almost adoration the people had for jazz and tap dance.

From the very first day in 1986 to the last day I was there in 2003, I have been greeted at the airport with flowers by Manu Collins, my producer, and students Kurt Albert and Klaus Blies (Tap & Tray). Manu, Kurt, and Klaus began their training with Carnell Lyons in Berlin. They were devoted to their master, and when I came to teach they invited Carnell to come to Nürnberg to look me over. Carnell not only came but, with his aged body and bad hip, took my class and then made the pronouncement that he was giving me his students, that they should continue their work with me. Then we drank so much cognac in a café that he missed his plane back to Berlin. There is much more ease in Europe, many more cognacs and coffees in cafés, and the students and performers there never tire of listening to tap stories.

In one of the festivals in Oregon, I met Christiana Sartorio from Milan, Italy. It was not long before I began to travel to Milan to stay at her apartment on San Andreas. There is something about Milan that makes me feel gauche even before I hit the street. Everyone is so perfectly put together, no wrinkles, no hanging threads — not the perfect place for a tap dancer to feel chic. But what a perfect place for me to make art because of Christiana and her friends, the brilliant jazz pianist Renato Sellani and bassist Massimo Morriconi. Everything about Italy is always an improvisation. I never know what will happen until I get there, and Christiana surprises me.

On one memorable occasion I was quite tired and quite grumpy. Why was I going to Italy anyway? Only one class had been set up and the students were notoriously disinterested. But when I arrived at Chris's apartment, she informed me that we were making a CD. She had arranged everything, and it happened immediately. Renato, Massimo, and I went into the recording studio at ten o'clock in the morning, and without a rehearsal came out with a finished product at one o'clock. I had always wanted to make a tap CD, and Chris produced the first one with two of my favorite musicians. She also produced Tony Waag and me, with Renato and Massimo, at the San Babilla Theater. It felt just as last minute and just as miraculous as everything else that happens to me in Italy.

For the first concert with the International Tap Dance Orchestra in Germany, Renato, with his girlfriend, Anna from Italy, Massimo, and Chris came to Nürnberg for our first rehearsal. Renato and Massimo were to be the musicians for a small tour arranged by Manu Collins and Winfried Hoffmann, two company members, in Düsseldorf and Wuppertal.

All the dancers had their music. There would be eleven acts, but when we began rehearsal we discovered that Renato didn't read music. It was orchestration by brail and humming. There was always high hysteria and much laughing as we rushed for trains and tried to navigate technical requirements in Italian, English, and German. After a while no one could converse plainly in any language, but we danced and played to new audiences everywhere.

In Berlin, I still teach at Ballet Centrum for Christian Toblenz and Thomas Fletcher. Also in Berlin, Cristina Delius and Anina Krueger's company name is Tapa Toe. Their school is one of the only schools in the world that offers only classes in tap dance. Every year I perform a one-person show at Café Theater Charlotte. Here in front of an enthusiastic German audience I try out new ideas and present material that is explorative and controversial. In collaboration with Cristina Delius, who is also a cellist as well as a tap dancer, we presented in 2002 a work with taps, cello, concertina, poetry, and piano, in response to the bombing of the World Trade Center.

I am not the only jazz musician or tap dancer who makes a big part of her living emotionally as well as materially in Europe. Michael Sandwick, an American tap dancer living in Copenhagen, recently starred and produced me in a tap show that ran for twelve consecutive nights with a vocal quartet, The Broadway Singers, and a band fronted by the outstanding Danish saxophone player Jesper Thilo and vocalist Ann Farholdt. Michael has a beautiful studio, performs regularly in theatrical productions, and, when he is not tap dancing, spends his time planting roses, stewing plums, and making apple sauce in his little home only fifteen minutes from downtown. Yes, working in Europe has offered me great artistic freedom as well as time to reflect, take a walk, and sit in the park viewing castles through flower gardens.

~

TWENTY

The Boomerang

COULD IT HAVE REALLY BEEN thirty hours long, this flight, this reentry, this suspension of time and gravity, the epic journey of once again returning home? The going, the leaving, the beginning of the journey never have the awe of an epic. I never want to go. Leaving home is abrasive, a tearing away of the skin. I have to cauterize the heart while I am in line to get my baggage checked. I am without anticipation.

No, it is the returning home that tasks this heroine – when the labyrinth of twisting tales try to tell themselves even when I don't want them to; when memory attached to the Rosella birds in fancy parrot plumage singing, talking, screeching in the palm trees on Auckland Street is more present than the air of actual time. The noisy birds flutter and fly in and out of my senses, which were just as vividly overwhelmed by the smell of eucalyptus on my first trip to the Dandenongs. I have taken that smell home with me, pungent and musty as my grandmother's top drawer of lace hankies nestled under a wad of potpourri. A flash through the mind, a clutch in my throat recall the roller coaster rumbling, carrying the screams of children still looking for a dare behind the open mouth of the gargoyle that is the front gate, the entrance of fear, to Luna Park in St. Kilda.

I'm carrying them with me, the people I have taught. Some are tucked safely into my luggage with the presents they gave me to take home: stuffed koala bears, a tiny stuffed wombat. Some of the students have penetrated even more deeply than my suitcase, have entered into my soul, where I will carry them with me for a long time. Even when I am finally home in body and spirit, snugly embraced by the heat of the wood-burning stove, Grant Swift will appear in his turned-backward, blue baseball cap (the only one I've ever seen without writing on it) and his well-worn, black, Funk Tap T-shirt with all the ribbing cut off. He will be tapping his Funk Tap rhythms under my beamed ceiling, pushing through the quiet as brash as an Aussie can be.

I have certainly carried him home with me, along with the mystery of why he chose to bring me, an aging female tap dancer, to Australia to teach his funk tap students the fine art of tone and texture. Grant, a bullyboy from New Zealand, was an ex-prizefighter, ex–male stripper, who liked nothing better than to tell me of his daredevil exploits and near death escapades. Why did he bring me so far from home to consult with and listen to my every word, learn my rhythms, and try to absorb my philosophy? He said it was because I made him cry when I went from my slow, soft *soft shoe* into my wild, fast Charles Mingus piece in 5/4.

So I will bring these mysteries to my New York homes and bury them all in the silence and darkness that will wrap around me like a woolly blanket itching with memories. For when I finally get there, that's what home is, a place where ghosts live when I am still and at rest, returned home like a boomerang from one country or town or one continent or another.

> *I wander from pillar to post*
> *Lost again out to sea*
> *Sometimes it seems*
> *That life has no seams*
> *Round and around I go*
> *Dancing my dance in another person's dream*

It is a progressive reentry, a homecoming as fragmented as my departures. Where is home? Is it New York City? Is it this apartment on Bethune Street, stretched out like a long bowling alley that I am invited to roll down when I open the door?

It is a fairly ordered space, semi-divided with living and working areas. The kitchen has coffee cups on open shelves next to salt and pepper shakers of glass blown in Corvallis, Oregon, by a tap student after the class I taught of sixty dancers in a roller skating rink. On the shelf over the sink is a bottle of cognac, purchased in some country I don't remember, next to a tea set I bought at a Turkish bazaar in Istanbul. In my office, my instructional videotapes and tap CDs line up neatly in a glass cabinet with books for sale. The contents of my catalog go out into the world without me. I can actually be in many places simultaneously ... Time Traveler.

The living room is also the bedroom, the dining room, the television room, the meditation room, and the video screening room. A big Baldwin upright piano given to the ATDO is secured against the wall. I can't play it in my apartment because it is too loud. Snuggled discreetly alongside the piano is my meditation shrine with stone Indian fetishes, a half-melted female Buddha candle, and incense brought back from a workshop trip to Winnipeg, Canada. Like fallen leaves blown by the wind, sheet music is lying in piles on the piano bench, on the little veneered dining table, on the rose chaise longue, and in a heap under the computer table. Evident everywhere is the chaos of my departure mind.

The eyes of my granddaughter Ella look intently from her photograph into the narrow room from the top of the piano where she rests next to a citation of recognition from the City of New York for my contributions to the field of tap dance. And right beside the piano, over the shrine, is the ten-foot-tall by three-foot-wide painting by my son Jeb. Abstract and wild, with horizons buried behind horizons, its surface is like a graveyard of broken ladders, with perspectives achieved by vivid gradations of color: yellow, maroon, blue, and green-blue. The painting is reflected by the mirror on the opposite wall, which also absorbs the view of the Empire State Building. I can see its reflection from my bed.

This tiny loft is my first home stop, a place to decide what to leave and what to take to my next home, or my next home away from home. I unpack the didgeridoo I bought at the Victoria Market in Melbourne. Its coarse, unsanded, hollowed-out tree branch decorated with yellow dots and red watering holes of the Aboriginal dreaming looks slightly off kilter balancing on the room divider. Beside it I place the woven hemp creature from New Guinea, created over a gourd, that Grant and his Tasmanian girlfriend, Melita, gave me on the last day of my trip.

The windup tin duck, wearing a perforated hat that spins when I've wound him up to ride his bicycle, waits expectantly. Cristina picked up the toy in the lounge of the Wintergarten Theatre in Berlin, where we went after rehearsal for our show of taps, cello, poetry, and concertina to watch a Christmas Cabaret of aerialists, jugglers, and tap dancers performing legomania in clown hats.

I repack the boomerang I brought from the Dandanongs for my grandson, Judah, my books on the Aboriginal Dream Time, ten opal pendant souvenirs, and two tea towels with Aboriginal designs to take them to my cottage work studio. The next house where I unpack to pack.

> *Somewhere . . . someone is singing my song*
> *If I hurry I might meet myself there*
> *A wanderer always seeking her home*
> *Dancing my dance in another person's dream*

In the car, all packed up with my repacked cases ... in the car, in a crunch with Jeb, my daughter-in-law, Celia, and my two tiny granddaughters, Alice and Ella. Celia is squashed between their car seats. I glance furtively back at them from time to time to gather their sweet essence. Alice was only one month old when I left. At two months she is bigger and pudgier, with eyes that see in which direction they are looking. Ella at three is completely occupying the image of herself, light, feathery as a sprite, and very gay. This is home, just being in their gaze. For a moment I feel that I exist. Their presence lights a fire that begins to warm the weary shell of the minstrel.

The Shawangunk Mountains hover in the distant haze. There is recognition of home in their steadfastness. But the eucalyptus trees of the Dandanongs were green and pungent. In contrast the maples and oaks of the New York forest stand naked and gray in their erect, stoic soldierliness, holding on against the war with winter. It is cold. Must I take the cold into me? Absorb the cold as home?

When Jeb drops me off and I drag my bags down the frozen path, I open the door to my cottage without much anticipation. I've been gone long enough to disconnect from this ancient dwelling in the woods and have made new and thorough connections with the waves lapping the course sand and porous rocks of St. Kilda. I expressed powerful vibrations into the steaming heat of the Phoenix Theatre, performing my one-person show and a new version of my newest tune, "About Face," as an Italian tango. I brought down the house, improvising for one hour straight with Steve Sedegreen's band at Dizzy's jazz club, dancing two sets on a three-foot-by-six-foot floor, surrounded by crowds sitting in chairs, leaning against the wall, perching on stools, and sitting shoulder to shoulder on top of the bar. At least twenty-five of them were my fan club of tap dancing women over sixty-five that followed me from venue to venue until I felt like the Mick Jagger of the geriatric set. That was warm, and the music was hot and my feet were flying, burning up the floor.

But here in the woods, in the kitchen of my cottage, it is cold and silent. Even the winter birds, the cardinals, the chickadees, and the nuthatches, are nowhere to be seen or heard. There are still dishes in the sink where I left them. Soggy green tea leaves in the cup have not gathered mold; it is too cold. Up the one step into the dining room, I am excited by the red wall I had painted for Christmas, but feel oppressed by the eight-foot ceilings which seem much lower than when I left. The armchair in the northern alcove by the three windows looking out on the little bamboo garden with the white Buddha – this Italian chair my mother gave me before she got Alzheimer's – looks incredibly empty. No vibration of the living left.

The little dining table in the southern alcove looks out at my dance studio and the wild dry branches of the forsythia bush, my barren vegetable garden, and the little forest. This dining table is at least one hundred and fifty years old, cracked and pockmarked as an old war veteran's face; this little table that I bought from my friend Steven for two hundred dollars is still scattered with Christmas cards, unopened mail, and unpaid bills. Under the clutter is the pottery candlestick holder, the one I made at our little studio down the road, covered with wax from the New Year's Eve party. The party's over and no voices linger over the half-empty bottles of wine that line the ceramic-tiled kitchen counter. Some of my plants are still green. My star begonias, the Christmas cactus, coleus, scraggly bougainvillea, and three jade plants are green but look limp, angry and intimidating. Leaves have fallen, dried and brittle on the Mexican tile floor. I set down my bags and begin the journey to the kitchen sink to water the dried out hibiscus and the parched gardenia plant.

I look in my black bag for eye drops. My eyes are stinging and aching. The back of my head is throbbing from lack of oxygen and whatever pressure is produced by not knowing what day it is or if I'm hungry, thirsty, tired, or ill. In the bag next to the eye drops is the last card written by Grant. It is a thank-you card with a photograph of him performing in our concert with his six-year-old son, Harry, dressed in a man's black dress suit, doing his *time step*, while his brother, four-year-old Oscar in his Winnie the Pooh shirt and baseball cap sings "It Don't Mean a Thing If It Ain't Got That Swing." I close my eyes and can hear the band come in on the "Do ... a Do ... a Do ... a" while the audience screams with pleasure.

I sit down for a minute on the old cherry chair next to the cold wood-burning stove in the living room and gaze at the portrait that my ex-husband painted of me and my infant son Zach thirty-nine years ago. A pair of left-behind black tap shoes tucked under the old pine hutch are the only visible link between my two worlds or three worlds or more. The tooled iron music stand that holds my concertina music is patiently waiting to be played when I finally return home in body and spirit. It is five o'clock. The sun sets, reflecting its colors over the brook. I will have to light the lights and the fire. In St. Kilda it would be time to take a walk on the beach or take a swim or have a coffee at a cake shop in the late afternoon warmth and sun.

> Now I come to this land of the setting sun
> Where songs of sparrows linger
> The darkening light beckons the night and only a shadow
>   malingers
> To dance her last dance in another person's dream

One More Time

Just when I think it all might be over, time to retire to my bamboo garden, something happens that moves me to another investigation or improvisation. This winter when I was traveling to Berlin, all my music got lost. I had to put a new show together in three days out of some Real Books the producer brought me from the library. Sitting on the smallest bed in the world, in the tiniest hotel room, while the gray sky offered only a relentless dreariness, I was reminded of those wonderful, lonely, frightened days alone on Burrill Street during the war, learning a song a day on the old piano. That weekend, with a brand new band, singing and dancing to a brand new repertory, I called the show "My Mother's Fake Book."

I never thought it would last this long. That at sixty-five I would still be traveling the globe as the oldest tap minstrel. The International and American Tap Dance Orchestras are not ensemble companies anymore, but Tony Waag, Margaret Morrison, and I still work on projects together.

We are at a full circle, beginning again. The American Tap Dance Orchestra's name has been changed to The American Tap Dance Foundation, and we are searching once again for a space to create a conservatory, to offer classes with a sustained developmental approach to bring students from beginner to professional level, as artists, dancers and musicians. Once again we are looking for performance space for new choreography, tap companies, and solo performances. We are at another moment, where we must jump-start the progress of our art form so that it will never disappear again. There is still so much to be done. Tap dance, in all its myriad colorations, has spread and is being developed around the globe, and I'm so happy to still be a part of that progress.

The life of a working tap dancer today is not much different than it has ever been. We are still meeting at airports and still trading stories and arguing over whose story is the real story.

PART TWO

Tap Techniques & Theory

Brenda Bufalino and Honi Coles giving a workshop in London with the great English clog dancer Sam Sherry (center).

~

TWENTY-ONE

Beyond Shuffle Ball Change

IN DISCUSSING TAP THEORY, I am assuming the dancer interested in my work has some experience. This section is not a
basic primer of how to do a *shuffle ball change* but rather a discussion of my technique and the technique of my mentor,
Honi Coles. It is also a story of our partnership as performers and teachers – how we learned to teach what we
once thought impossible to teach.

As tap dancers, we are still creating our form; it is still
developing; that's what makes it so exciting. Tap dance as
an art form is far from finished.

I have always been interested in developing techniques
that help dancers become their own teachers and develop
their uniqueness – methods that help dancers identify and
refine their own style and sound. Learning a dictionary full
of steps does not make a tap dancer. It is a deep and arduous search entailing many hours of practice, alone, listening
to your tap as it hits the floor.

Every dancer starts out with very unique movements
and has his or her own style. But sometimes, with all the
studying and copying, it's hard to remember or discover

what that style is. With self-study and a critical eye and ear, each of us must be our own teacher.

Instructors can help their students develop an inner eye and ear in order to answer the calls of their souls. I can teach students my manipulations and footwork, but more importantly I can encourage self-observation. Seeing what we don't know gives us the opportunity to work with a beginner's mind. If we wrap our ideas too tightly, we can kill them rather than let them evolve and expand.

• *The hardest students to teach are the ones who think they know everything already.*

IDENTIFYING YOUR SOUND

• *The sound of your taps is like the sound of your voice: a signature.*

Honi had a particular way of hitting the floor with a tap that distinguished his sound, just as I have my own attack that produces a recognizable tone. Every dancer has a sound whether he or she has decided to develop it consciously or not.

In 1978 when I climbed the stairs to Jerry Leroy's studio on 8th Avenue between 46th and 47th Streets, I could hear Honi warming up in preparation for our rehearsal, and I could always identify the light sound of his taps; they rang through the din of other dancers' taps, castanets, and cymbals that filled the air. His taps sang — soft they sounded, and engaging, drawing you to them, making you listen, and then suddenly exploding. He usually wore a plain Capezio oxford and would let his Morgan or Tele Tone metal taps shave down to a sliver. There was nothing fancy about his equipment. Clarity, acoustic resonance, and dynamics were his focus.

After teaching for so many years on so many continents, I have developed a method for producing a tap. Though it is a method of ease, it wasn't easy to develop. I banged, I prodded, I dug at the floor, I slammed the floor. I thought if I used all my energy, a beautiful tone would develop. What developed instead was arthritis and gout caused by the intense pressure I was putting on my feet along with the anxiety and desire for perfection that was tensing my muscles. It took many years of experimentation before I discovered how to use my body to help produce the sound from the feet with the least amount of effort.

• *Keep the body relaxed; relaxation is the key to producing beautiful tones as well as keeping the time "in the pocket."*

When you relax you can feel the floor, not just with the feet but with the whole body. When you tense, your muscles shorten. When you relax, they lengthen; they get heavier and just fall into place.

• *Feel your bones and sense that your legs are twelve feet long.*

When confronted with a new class and students always eager for a new step, my first response is that you have to learn how to tap dance by developing manipulations of the foot as rudiments that are repeated in many different configurations and speeds.

For the tap dancer the practice of rudiments and methods of articulation can be compared to the training and practice of a pianist working on scales and chord progressions. The student needs to understand how to use the rudiments that go into making up a step in many different ways, for many different phrases or figures, in many different time signatures and tempos.

• *It takes too long to learn to tap by memorizing one routine a year for a recital.*

The accumulation and practice of manipulations is also the key to improvisation. Having facility, the composer can then create spontaneously, can free the mind to connect with the voice and sing melodies and rhythms through the feet without constriction.

Because I have always had problems with attention, not to mention a very rebellious spirit, I have never been able to memorize. This handicap produced a great benefit. Because I could not remember steps I always had to improvise, and I always created my own material. Except for historical vernacular routines like the "Shim Sham Shimmy" or "The Old Soft Shoe" or the choreography that Honi and I performed in our concerts together, I never performed solo with another dancer's steps.

What I have absorbed from my teachers or favorite dancers are manipulations (ways to produce a tap), which I collect greedily. Every time I find a new way of moving my foot, a new way to produce a sound, a new configuration of movement that makes a shape, I return to the studio for hours of practice.

I also pride myself on the amount of manipulations I have been able to invent and develop that uniquely express my style. The more manipulations I master, the more vitality, ingenuity, and musicality there is to my improvisation. It is as if I have letters to make sentences with, and those sentences make up my dance story.

The dance story, or composition, is improvisation that has been captured, pruned, and refined. Eventually, in order to polish my compositions with definition and refinement, I had to train myself to memorize some of my own material. But it is through the freedom of spirit that an individual voice is realized.

In the mid-1970s, when Honi and I collaborated in teaching tap dance, we had to begin from scratch. Many of the students we encountered had never tapped before or had received instruction that stuck them to the ground rather than moved them across the floor – or they had stiff bodies poised in a ballet *port de bras*. From this formal position it was not possible to express the rhythm in a physically relaxed way. We soon discovered that if the body was not relaxed the dancer could not express the phrase dynamically or even accurately.

Honi and I learned to teach by studying the success or failure of our students. We, too, had to begin at the beginning, at the beginning of the tap revival.

ARTICULATING FLAPS

When Honi and I began teaching students together, our first moment of elated realization about the actualization of a *flap* came during one of the tap classes at The Dancing Theatre. We were watching the dancers trying to create a sound with their *flaps* while barely lifting their legs. They brought the action from behind and did not lift the knee up in the front.

The action for a *flap* or a *slap* is similar to a *prance*.
- *Lift the knee directly in front and release the foot in a relaxed manner to articulate two beats as it strikes the floor.*
- *At the last moment change your weight so the foot has a tight landing and doesn't slide.*

We were ecstatic over this discovery of how to teach a *flap* because it very often sets the tempo for the band. This manipulation needs to be absolutely clear with its rhythm, persistent and never fluctuating. Changing the weight on each *flap* sets the pulse throughout the body and makes the rhythm visual. Students were soon coming to our workshops from all over the country to learn fast footwork; they often found themselves executing *flaps* for an entire class.

To deepen your understanding, consider the following:

- *Each speed has its own action. The slower the tempo, the higher the leg action: Imagine the leg is twelve feet long.*
- *The faster the tempo the less action there is from the leg.*
- *Finally, at top speed the foot hardly leaves the ground and a flap becomes a brush ball.*
- *Do not lift the foot to the back to make a flap.*
- *Practice flaps traveling backwards like Bill "Bojangles" Robinson. This forces the leg into the correct high frontal position.*

It is said that Bill Robinson, affectionately called Uncle Bo by tap dancers, would challenge people to a race, with them running forward while he ran backward. In many of his famous routines Uncle Bo syncopates *flaps* while traveling backwards in his elegant, straight-back posture.

(Refer to instruction tape *Where The Action Is*.)

The Swing Groove

When Honi and I taught our first workshop together in New York City in the late 1970s, I was surprised to find that there were only ten tap dancers interested in rhythm tap and that, except for Henry LeTang, there were no other teachers of this style. But our first workshop led to the next generation of professionals, still working today.

These dancers did not grow up with jazz. They had no idea of how to distinguish jazz rhythms and syncopation from straight time. One of the immediate challenges in teaching this enthusiastic group was to get them to swing. We had to figure out how to teach them to swing, how to create an understanding so they wouldn't rush the time and push the beat. The search for this understanding took many more years of experimentation before success was achieved. My answer to this question is to establish the groove and dance inside of it.

Establishing a Swing Groove with Flaps in 4/4 Time

Because *flaps* can establish a groove as well as a tempo, placing a clap on the *two* and the *four* beat of the four-bar phrase establishes a swing groove.

Singing the accent of a *long one* and a short *pushed three* of the four-bar phrase gives the "back up" solid drive of a Charleston beat.

• *Great dancers do not have good rhythm, they have good rhythms.*

The more rhythms the dancer can hold in his or her body while clapping, singing, flapping, and swinging the arms in a relaxed manner, the more "in the pocket" the rhythm will be. Consider the complexity of multiple rhythms that the traps drummer plays simultaneously. Each module of the kit is played with a different rhythm. The bass drum, the high hat, the cymbal, the snare drum, the tom-toms make up the density and driving patterns of the time signature that the rest of the band depends on for keeping time.

- *When the flap action for the tempo is precise and when the dancer holds many rhythms in his or her body simultaneously, the tempo remains consistent, not rushed or falling behind.*

Simultaneous Group Improvisation with Flaps

One half of the dance class is the band, holding the *flap* groove for four bars, while the other half of the class simultaneously improvs over the groove. Then the roles reverse; the groove group improvs and the improv group holds the groove. Then the improvisation is extended to eight bars of *flaps* and eight bars of improv. You can stay with this improvisation for many choruses.

Three-way Listening

- *Listen to yourself from the head down through the center of your body.*
- *Don't lean with your head down to hear your sound; it won't help.*
- *Don't try to block out the other dancers; you will just get louder and not be in relationship to the rest of the group.*
- *Listen to the dancers on your left and right.*
- *Include the music in your listening.*

When you can include the entire ensemble in your listening, with yourself at the center, you can make appropriate musical choices. You will experience the sweet sensation of musicianship when adding to the musicality of the whole, accenting or complimenting when necessary, holding time, or soloing when the space arises.

- *Feel the body in the dance. Don't let your energy carry you away.*
- *Energy and feeling have different qualities. Don't substitute energy for feeling. Feel the beat.*
- *Use the appropriate energy for each execution and groove.*

FLAPS, CLAPS & THE GROOVE

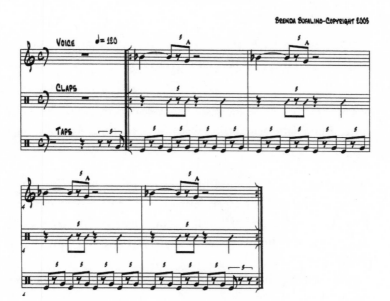

- *A swing groove is relaxed and easy. Energy is used for dynamic changes and accents.*

After a groove has been firmly established, executing manipulations and learning combinations will proceed easily without coaxing from the teacher on the sideline saying, "You're rushing ... you're rushing." This work on the groove, developed and refined over many years, will hold dancers back from their headlong drive to push the beat.

- *If you don't collect a horse at a canter, it will run away with you. If you don't include sensation and multiple rhythms in your body and mind, the tempo will run away with you.*
- *Never work mechanically while doing technique or rudiments. Do not wait to dance — dance every moment, invest every manipulation with conscious engagement.*

(Refer to instruction tapes *Where the Action Is* and *St. Valentines Day Waltz.*)

THE SHUFFLE SCALE

These are the *shuffle* exercises I developed for melody and tone. The *shuffle* offers the greatest opportunity for singing with your taps. The cultivation of tonal execution is essential in creating compositions for ensemble. I particularly like an ensemble to sound like one person tapping. That is not possible if everyone is hitting a different part of the foot on a *shuffle* and with different energies. When every dancer hits the high note of a *shuffle* at the same time, it is like an orchestra of violins.

Controlling the changing dynamics of the shuffle helps to make a distinction between the treble (toe) and the bass (heel) of a phrase, especially as it develops into counterpoint.

Here are some thoughts to keep in mind as you travel through these positions:

* *Let the leg, the hip, the pelvis, and the buttocks do the work.*
* *Keep the foot relaxed but the focus exact.*
* *Hear the sound before you try to execute it, just as you would hear a note before you sing it.*

Six different positions on the toe tap are used to create the six-note scale.

* *The first position or tone is hit with the heel shuffle.*

The note is a neutral sound without resonance. Do not bend the standing leg to reach the heel. Stretch the working leg to reach the heel.

- *The second position is on the tip of the toe.*

It is our highest note and our lightest application. You cannot get a high note with force. The torso is lifted out of the hip of the working leg and the hip is slightly raised. The *shuffle* is aimed directly forward.

- *The third position is a circular shuffle, which is also executed from the tip of the toe.*

It is our next-to-highest note and also has a light application. The whole leg creates a circle counterclockwise. The foot is also working in this exercise to create the counterclockwise circle. It might be wise to practice this slowly, exercising the ankle through the desired position. The speed of developing this facility is different for everyone and depends on how loose or tight a particular ankle is. At first it might seem awkward, but after time, with the aid of the hip, the manipulation and tone should release with ease. This position is very useful for executing *shuffles* with speed.

- *The fourth position is the most awkward and is a medium-range note.*

It is initiated by striking the outside of the foot and is brought back by striking the inside, as if you were scraping something off the two sides of your foot. This is a dark tone and uses a forceful initiation so that the back swing almost happens by itself. The hip cannot help you with this manipulation and there is some strain in the pelvis as it is asked to do the impossible of expanding and contracting. This position is very useful in developing the scrape for a *single wing* and also useful for developing the *five-tap wing.*

- *The fifth position is struck on the fat part of the tap.*

This is the most natural and accessible position. If the entire leg initiates the action, a fat, loud *shuffle* hits a note in the midrange. A good solid rebound will make the tap ring.

SHUFFLE SCALE

- *The sixth and last position is the darkest tone, a woody sound almost like a knock.*

It is executed with the leg out directly to the side and the *shuffle* applied to the inside of the shoe. Hitting the sound on the leather sole makes a deep and rich tone. A good solid rebound makes the tone and dynamic consistent. This position is also very useful for developing speed.

- *Execute shuffles in each position eight times down scale, four times up.*
- *Execute in each position two times down the scale and two times up. (Repeat twice.)*
- *Execute once in each position, once down the scale and once up. (Repeat three times.)*

Striking the *shuffle* once in each position is quite difficult to maneuver. Don't slow down or change speeds as you go along. Allow yourself to struggle with the slow response of the synapse. Just keep relaxing the mind, stay in motion, maintain the tempo, and hit as many taps as you can correctly. Eventually the synapse will begin to make connections. Developing quick reactions from the synapse is necessary for utilizing these techniques within a phrase. Of course, the exercise is executed on the right and left side.

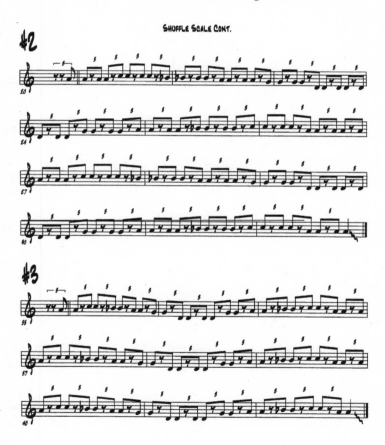

SHUFFLE SCALE CONT.

TRIPLET SHUFFLES

While executing the *triplet shuffles,* maintain your relation-ship to the tone in each position. The rhythms can be exe-cuted consecutively. It will be necessary to practice the first and the fourth positions at slower tempos because of the degree of difficulty.

- *Again, you must hear the note before you execute it.*
- *In the first four positions of the scale the triplet shuffle starts on "a four and a one." The accent is on the "one" of each phrase, on the for-ward motion of the shuffle.*
- *Take aim precisely and apply the dynamics consistently in each phrase.*
- *On the last two positions of the scale, the triplet shuffle starts on "four and a one." The "one" accent is now to the back and is executed with more force from the entire leg.*

The *break* of this exercise is in the continuation. Of course, the exercises must be executed on both sides.

Playing Eighth Notes on a Seven-Beat Phrase

I like to finish this *shuffle* series with *brush, heel, shuffle-ball-heel, dig* (R, L R, L); *brush, heel, shuffle-ball-heel, dig* (L, R L, R), etc., repeated over and over in straight eighth notes and then in straight sixteenth notes. Repeating this seven-beat sequence at different tempos and in different time frames informs me of my speed and accuracy and tunes up my rhythmic and melodic ear.

First, execute this combination with no syncopation or dynamics, very delicately, until the space between the notes is consistent. Then repeat the repetitions bringing up the

EIGHTH NOTE TRIPLET SHUFFLES
EXECUTE ON RIGHT AND LEFT

volume in the heels for a clave counterpoint and syncopation that lives inside the figure and emerges like a mystery revealed.

- *Stay relaxed. Lift the rib cage for light sounds, but don't lift or tense the shoulders.*
- *To achieve a high tone from the tap, hit the very tip of the tap very softly. The more force, the darker and deeper the tone.*

  (Refer to instruction tape *Where the Action Is.*)

PLAYING 8TH NOTES ON A 7-BEAT PHRASE

SMALL FOOTWORK EXCERCISES

I like to develop my figures with intricate footwork — *crawls, riffs* — and a variety of rhythm turns that create long extended bebop phrases that do not repeat. These phrases might duplicate the melody of the tune I'm dancing to or create an a cappella rhythmic melody or dance over an improvisation with the pianist or bass player.

I like to work contrapuntally, with the pianist playing phrases with the right hand and eliminating the block chords or bass line from the left hand. This allows me to dance lightly and have my patterns easily heard over the piano melodies.

I don't particularly like trades, though I use them occasionally. I prefer a light instrumentation and soloing simultaneously with band members. I also like to start off slow and double the time, triple the time, even double the triple if I haven't set the initial tempo too fast.

For all this footwork I have developed exercises to create long runs of phrases. These exercises give me the confidence that all of my manipulations will be consistent in tempo. I warm up with these exercises before every show. I like to know before I hit the spotlight how clean and fast my chops are.

I also enjoy working in a variety of time signatures, like a slow waltz in 3/4, or a driving 6/8, or a more modern 5/4 or 7/8. Having the capacity to switch from swing to bop, from Latin to classical, keeps me working. I always have something to pull out of my hat if a show is overloaded with fast dancers or slow dancers. So naturally it is important to practice these exercises in all different time signatures.

All of these manipulations are executed with an initiation from the hip. A certain bounce given to the execution helps to spring the foot back into action when a cycle has been completed. Though all the small muscles in the bottom of the foot are called to action, the foot must be relaxed following the momentum from the hip initiation.

These manipulations begin in single time and move to double time with a double time continuation. Choose a single time slow enough for you to double with a little effort. Always finish a cycle of exercises faster than you can do them. In your final run you will probably miss as many taps at double time as you make. The object is to build momentum, to tell your body and your feet what you expect of them in the near future. Begin clean and precise; eventually end up dancing so fast there are only air taps. Tap faster than you can execute; don't make adjustments.

First Exercise
- *The action is initiated from the hip. Manipulation begins on "and a one": Brush in-ball-heel* (R). *The "one" is on the heel.*
- *Don't tighten the toes. When they start to tighten, talk to them gently and release them.*
- *Don't slow down on the double time. You can't learn to dance fast by dancing slow.*

Repeat three times and then execute a double time continuation for four bars. Repeat on the left side.

Second Exercise
- *Brush in, ball-heel heel* (R, R L). *The left heel is now the "one."*

Repeat three times on right foot and then execute double-time continuation for four bars.

Third Exercise
- *Release the right leg to the front and rock the body back and forth as if you are on a horse. Lean back to prepare.*
- *Dig-brush-ball-heel* (R). *The "one" is on the heel.*

Repeat as in one and two and repeat whole exercise on the left.

Fourth Exercise
Same as the third exercise, but adding the left heel.
- *Dig-brush-ball-heel, heel* (R, L). *The "one" is on the left heel*

Repeat the single time and double time on the left foot.

SMALL FOOTWORK EXERCISES
EXECUTE ON RIGHT AND LEFT

With the completion of these exercises the feet should be warmed up for the execution of double-time figures, paddle and rolls, and crawls.

(Refer to instruction tape *Where the Action Is*.)

SMALL FOOTWORK EXERCISES

SMALL FOOTWORK EXERCISES

DEVELOPING PATTERNS FOR PHRASING AND DOUBLE TIME

Sometimes we are stopped dead in our tracks, think we might quit, and wonder what the point is. This is the moment to really look deeply and find a new answer to old questions.

This has happened to me many times in my career. At one point in my early career I was really stuck, repeating myself over and over in my *double time* improvisations. It was always the same old *paddle and roll . . . paddle and roll . . . roll and paddle.* I needed to develop combinations that were suitable for both exclamation points and fast continuations. I needed more variety in the way I used my feet and traveled across the floor. Self-study was the only answer. I couldn't study anyone else. Everyone else had the same problem. I saw that they were also very repetitive and predictable.

Even Honi entered his exclamation points with the same footwork all the time. I could anticipate what he was going to do next. I didn't want to be limited to one or two patterns. Perhaps the answer lay in the way I moved into my rhythms.

I remembered an old review I had received for my Afro-Cuban act in *Variety* magazine. The reviewer called my movements "serpentine," and I thought perhaps that was a clue. As I studied my visual as well as audio presentation, I saw that many of my figures had *crawls* in them; I was serpentine with my feet as well as my body. From these I extrapolated particular close-to-the-floor *crawls* that I used in a rhythm, practicing these serpentine patterns until I could execute each continuation with absolute clarity and facility.

The study of tap dance is the study of natural laws such as these:

- *If I pull my body away from my feet I can pick them up faster.*
- *If my foot is placed too far to the right or left, too far forward or backward, I get no profit even if I practice the same manipulation for weeks or even years.*
- *I study the big muscles and the small. If improvement is not made right away I shift my weight and adjust my action.*

With a disclaimer, I am transcribing a few of my double time exercises to paper. I don't really believe it is possible to read a tap rhythm from a paper, but since some people think they can understand it, I am making this attempt. I am also making a melodic notation of the single *paddle and roll* with the *double paddle break* exercise available. This gives a tonal interpretation as well as rhythmic.

All of these double-time exercises for speed and accuracy can be swung or played in straight sixteenth notes to create fast phrases. These patterns can also be played slowly in single time as eighth notes. All the exercises can be transposed into eighth note triplets.

I feel as if I am singing with my taps. These exercises keep me tuned up.

Basic Paddle and Roll with a Double Paddle Break

The whole phrase is 8 bars. Begin on the right. Repeat five times, RLRLR.

- *brush–in ball heel   dig brush ball heel*
           R   L

DOUBLE TIME EXERCISE
SINGLE PADDLE WITH DOUBLE PADDLE BREAK

BRENDA BUFALINO—COPYRIGHT 2005

- *dig brush ball heel   dig brush ball heel   dig brush ball heel*

  R   L   R
- *dig brush dig brush ball heel   dig brush dig brush ball heel*

  L   R

Execute the whole pattern right, left, and right. Then execute a two-bar continuation of five *double paddles* ending with a *heel toe* on the right.

Paddle and Roll with Shuffle Variation

Eight-bar phrase:
- *brush heel   shuffle ball heel   dig brush ball heel*

  R L   R   L
- *dig brush dig brush ball heel*

  R
- *dig brush dig brush ball heel*

  L

- *dig brush   heel   shuffle-ball-heel   dig brush step*
  R   L   R   L
- *heel   dig brush dig brush ball heel*
  L   R
- *dig brush dig brush ball heel*
           L
- *dig brush dig brush ball heel*
           R
- *dig brush dig brush ball heel*
           L
- *dig brush heel   brush step*
  R   L   R

Repeat the figure on the left side.

When Honi and I rehearsed together, he created most of the material we performed together. He was six foot three and had very long legs. I was five foot three with much shorter legs. I often blamed my inability to pick up one of his manipulations on the fact that I had shorter legs. He, as usual, was not interested in why I couldn't to it, only that I must.

One day in desperation I walked around him and studied his body while he was executing a very fast figure. I saw that his hips and pelvis were initiating the movement. It was very subtle; he didn't even know that this was true. I began to use a rocking pelvis motion when I practiced some *crawls* that involved lifting the toe in the front. Not only did I increase my speed, but I didn't get shin splints. When I practiced without the rocking motion I very quickly felt a strain in my shins. Shin splints take months to heal. It is advisable to never let the shins get too tired.

Rocking the hips ever so slightly lifts the toes off the ground, so the shin muscle doesn't have to do the work. This frees up the feet so that you can articulate a subtle move with speed.

The connections with the synapse necessary to execute a different pattern with the right and the left foot simultaneously can be strengthened only by repetition. For instance, executing a *toe-heel* continuation on the left foot while the right foot is executing *dig-toe* is equivalent to the game of patting your head and rubbing your stomach at the same time.

I have named the next *two* crawls simply to differentiate them. They have no real names, and these are not used by anyone but me.

The Swampscott Crawl

Eight-bar phrase traveling to the left:
- *dig brush ball heel   dig brush ball heel*

       R   L
- *toe toe heel heel   toe toe heel heel*

    R L R L   R L R L

Repeat three times for six bars with a two-bar continuation *break* ending on the right toe.
- *Rock slightly off the toes as you crawl along.*
- *When traveling to the left always lead with the right foot on the crawl.*
- *When traveling to the right always lead with the left foot.*
- *Keep your head up. If you drop your head to look at your feet it's harder to pick up your toes.*
- *In a syncopated phrase you do not have to follow this specific direction. It is only necessary to have a lead foot if you are doing repetitions.*

The Shawangunk Crawl

This is a twelve-bar phrase; for faster speed lean body away from the working foot.

- *brush heel   shuffle ball heel   dig brush ball heel*

    R   L   R   L

- *dig brush ball heel toe heel toe*

            R

- *brush ball heel   dig brush ball heel toe heel toe   brush ball heel*

       L   R   L

- *brush step heel toe heel   brush ball heel*

       L   R

- *brush step heel toe heel   brush ball heel*

       L   R

- *brush step heel toe heel   brush ball heel*

       L   R

- *brush step heel toe heel   brush ball heel*

       L   R

- *brush step heel toe   brush step*

       L   R

- *brush step heel toe heel   brush ball heel*

       L   R

- *brush heel toe   brush step*

     L   R

- *Execute a four-bar continuation of the first idea and repeat the whole twelve-bar phrase beginning on the left foot.*

(Refer to these exercises in the instruction tape *Double Time Series*.)

Time Steps

In 1944, when I was seven years old, the linoleum kitchen floor at 211 Burrill Street was worn thin by my daily practice. I practiced all the time. As soon as I learned a *shuffle ball change*, as soon as I had something to express, I expressed it — all the time.

My mother, Marjorie, was also very expressive. From the time I was eight until I was eleven years old, she was working in nightclubs or doing club dates around Boston, Lowell, Lawrence, and Revere Beach. With her beautiful lyric soprano voice and her flowing, honey-colored hair, she wrapped the audience in longing as she sang sad songs like "Smoke Gets In Your Eyes" and "Willow Weep for Me."

She brought people home from her gigs late at night, and I'd get out of bed, rub my eyes, and show off my *Shuffle Off To Buffalo*. On one particularly cold winter night she brought home two comedians for a cup of tea. They were quite well known; I think their names were Martin and Rossi. Of course, there were so many acts in those days, and the names were so similar, it was hard to keep track. Anyway, it was a defining moment in my youthful career.

The smaller, fatter, dark-curly-haired comedian asked to see my *time step.* Eager to oblige, I showed the only one I knew, the one everybody knew: *hop shuffle step a flap ball change,* or as I heard Ernest "Brownie" Brown call it years later, *thank you for the buggy ride.*

"Oh!" Rossi said. "That's so corny and old-fashioned. I'll show you a much hipper *time step.*" In his dark brown loafers he set himself solidly into the floor and laid out the most fabulous rhythms in a *time step* I had ever heard. In fact, what he showed me was the *rhythm time step* in 4/4 time, which was more spacious and syncopated than my *time step* in 2/4. This *time step* was breezy and, to my young impressionable ears, seemed to go on and on forever.

"Sha do be dop … badoo badee badop … Sha do ba do be dop," he sang, accenting each *dop* deliberately and emphatically with a stamp. "See — that swings," he said.

I worked on that *time step* long after Martin and Rossi had gone home and my mother had fallen asleep on the sofa.

The *time step* is the foundation of traditional routines. All tap dancers know at least one *time step.* Tap dancers on the vaudeville circuit had bragging rights about how many *time steps* they had created.

"I've got twenty four *time steps.*"

"Well that ain't nothin' — I've got forty four."

- Time steps *are primarily about setting the time, and keeping the time; creating a groove for what is to follow as well as the style the dancer will be working in.*

Until the 1950s most tap compositions were called routines. A routine was usually short and sweet. Vaudeville acts had about twelve minutes to say all they had to say.

- *Most routines were a series of different* time steps *with the same break, or the same* time step *with different breaks.*

- *Today* time steps *are often incorporated into a long composition of extended phrases. It is a rhythm to which the improviser will return periodically to lock in the time, reestablish the time, or set up the next step or figure.*

- *A one-bar* time step *repeats six times and ends with a fancy two-bar break.*

- *A two-bar* time step *repeats three times and culminates with a two-bar resolution.*

Or:

- *A* time step *is a reference point with an indeterminate amount of repetitions.*
- *The* time step *sets the body in motion.*
- *The repetitive* time step *synchronizes the dancer's body with the voice and puts the system in right relationship to itself.*
- Time steps *have a calm and unifying effect, like a child's nursery rhyme . . . like a poem.*
- *The* time step *is the prelude to the expression that is to follow.*
- *You can ride a* time step *for a while with ease and get into the groove.*
- *Settle yourself.*
- *Know where you are.*
- *Tell others where you are. Tell the band, your partner, your audience, and your feet where you are.*

There is nothing more exasperating then listening to a dancer lose the time on a *time step* or not know where the "one" of a four-beat measure falls each time in the step or how the step sits over the measure. A *time step* must maintain the groove and be secure and steady, or it has no reason for being.

Basic Rhythm Time Step

- *stamp stamp stamp stomp brush-step stomp-brush-step stomp*
  L   R   L   R   R   L   R
- *flap flap flap*
  R   L   R

  Repeat three times.
  Break:
- *stamp stamp stamp stomp*
  L   R   L   R

- *brush   step stomp brush step   stomp brush step   stomp brush step*
  R   L   L   R   R   L
- *stomp*
  R

The Short Rhythm

After years of addressing the students' problem of rushing the time, I developed a technique for hearing a short rhythm within the longer phrase. The short rhythm of a step is accentuated by the bass sound of the *heel* — or a dynamic *stamp*. I also call this the "backbeat" of a step. It defines how the step sits over the time or how the bass note sits in back of the treble. The treble is produced by the toe, and the bass by the *heel* or a *stomp*.

A drummer has a full kit to help define the short rhythms; the bass drum keeps a steady beat, while the cymbal, high hat, and snare drum multiply the rhythms. Tap dancers only have two feet, so we try to divide the foot into a full drum kit, using the heel as the bass drum. Even in the most intricate of steps this short rhythm of the heel or stamp (like a clave beat in a Latin band) drives home the essentials.

- *Perhaps your* time step *has five taps; the backbeat may shine through with three dominant beats.*
- *Where these three primary beats sit in the measure is the ring of the step; the bass rhythm, and all else flurries on top of it in right proportion.*
- *Every phrase has a shorter phrase within it where the accents are placed, and they stay there, repeated precisely each time. Now you know where you are, and the band knows where you are.*

I repeat, if the time is not clear on a *time step* — clear and swinging — there is no sense in doing one at all.

More Thoughts on Composing with Time Steps

• *If the* time step *is extended longer than eight bars, it sets a looser structure for the composition.*
• *There are* time steps *in different modes and time signatures: swing, bebop, rumba, mambo, soft shoe, blues, waltz, etc.; 2/4, 4/4, 3/4, 5/4, 6/8, etc.*

Sometimes in a more contemporary approach the *time step*, after being presented once, hides in the background like a memory lingering. In this vein you allow for changes and for the unexpected segue into tempo and mode changes. These ideas can work as interruptions or subtle rhythmic breakdowns of the time until a new theme is established.

In the very sophisticated genre of modern jazz tap, the *time step* often disappears altogether. Nevertheless, the dancer's first statement signifies what the dance will say. Here the dancer is working with extended phrases, weaving the story like a tapestry, using subtleties of expression and texture that often can only be experienced but not recognized by the untrained eye or, more significantly, the ear. There are as many ideas for *time steps* as there are melodies for a song.

From the 1970s to the present, improvisational performances, innovated by the late Baby Lawrence in the bebop era, have often been presented on the concert stage and in performance tap jams. But even here the *time step* has a place. It is still home, a place to leave for a long or short journey, a place to come back to, to regroup or set out on a new course.

When you are creating your dance the *time step* sets the theme, sets the mode as well as the time. You may perform it only once, but you know it is there as the backbone of the composition.

(Refer to videotape *Great Feats of Feet: Portrait Of A Jazz Tap Dancer* and instruction tape *Tap Intensive 1*.)

Structures For Improvisation

As Jimmy Slyde would say, "It's not possible to teach improvisation." Of course not: if you were taught it, it wouldn't be spontaneous. But there are structures to consider that can offer a context and a platform for invention. My personal challenge is to present clear articulation and compositional development while improvising so that my performance has the freshness of improvisation with the sophistication of a well-rehearsed composition.

To compose while you are improvising becomes distinct from making up a routine or simply paraphrasing steps you already know. Listening to musicians playing live, you expand your perceptions and become aware that the soloists, when they are improvising, are coming from somewhere and going somewhere, not just playing licks. There is structure to improvisation just as there is structure in composition. If you set out a statement, you must follow it through. You might ask, "What was that statement anyway? After the sixteenth bar I can't remember it."

Finally you stand in awe at the complexity of mastering the art of improvisation. There are many elements. The mind must be quick and the feet absolutely connected to the mind, as quick as a thought or an emotion, with no hesitation. It is akin to telling a story off the top of your head with a beginning, middle, and end. There must be surprises so that the listeners do not go to sleep, dreaming their own rhythms instead of yours. You must know musical structure and time signatures – the ability to always know, while improvising, where you are in the music and to be able to merge again into the theme. There is no time to think; it must become second nature, intuitive.

While it's important for jazz tap dancers to improvise from the very start of their careers, it is also important to start on this journey with humility and realize that it is a long road to freedom. Technique and knowledge have to keep pace with the desire to bust out. Tap dance is noisy and can easily become extraneous sound, just a trick, a novelty that always gets a hand. Therein lies the intrinsic danger of the form.

Working off a Time Step

Performing tap dancers still in training will often come to me for work on improvisation. I first ask them to show me some of their *time steps*. It is surprising how few of them have any solid *time steps* of their own or even have any *time steps* at all. That is akin to a jazz musician who has a thousand licks but doesn't know any tunes. So I will give dancers a *time step* and ask them to improvise off of it, stay in the mode that they have started and then return to their initial step. Perhaps it's a *time step* of six bars and a two-bar *break* and an eight-bar improvisation, then back to the *time step* on exactly the right beat and on exactly the right part of the phrase of music.

Then the improvisation sections can be extended. You can make a conscious decision to segue into a new mode, move into half time or double time, and then abruptly, precisely, return to the original time. Keeping track of all the elements at play in your improvisation helps you to guide your work to its conclusion in a way that makes sense. But, remember, the band plays on, and if you are dancing with them, you have to know where they are.

This is the excitement of improvisation – so many parts of the brain, heart, body, and feet, simultaneously creating with knowledge and intuition, keenly aware of every opportunity, hearing all of the subtleties of the other musicians so that a dialogue is created. One organism, one body of music.

• *Improvise playing eighth notes.*

As you did at the end of the *shuffle* section, practice playing all your manipulations and continuations as straight eighth notes, very clean and clear.

• *Sometimes make these notes very staccato, sometimes swing them.*

Execute these eighth note improvs very quietly, without accents from the heel, until they are perfectly clear and then double them, maintaining the tone and texture of the notes and the consistency of the space between them. Then switch from single to double time, or into triplets, remembering the idea of hesitation and anticipation. Listen gently to your sound, your clear speed and perfect continuity.

When and if a degree of perfection is achieved, bring up the volume of the heels to present a counter rhythm and syncopation inside your eighth- or sixteenth-note repetitions. Unexpected rhythms will appear, emerging from the inside out. Maintain your connection to the straight eighth notes or you will lose the irregular syncopation to a symmetrical rhythm, one you already know.

• *Work with peripheral vision.*

"How can I keep from repeating the same phrases when I improvise?" To answer this question it might be useful to examine why we repeat and feel like a broken record. Often I find it is because I am closed off from external influences. My focus is so tight that all I can see or feel is the tip of my nose. To escape this prison of limited ideas and perpetual run-on-tap-sentences going nowhere, it helps to increase my peripheral vision and take my eyes off the floor. I notice the color of the room, the crack in the window, the tree waving in the wind outside, the airplane noise.

- *What I take in with my senses from my environment will increase my options for response.*

While I am dancing in some old rehearsal studio I can notice a hole that someone kicked through the wall or the peeling paint and dead flowers in a vase. I can see the circumference of the room and move through it. I take myself out of my two-by-two-foot cage and reach far out in space with my body and my rhythms. By expanding my physical limitations, I can reach for the ceiling, reach to touch the two sides of the room, increasing my personal magnetism and charisma.

- *I'm aware of the other dancers on the stage or in the studio with me.*

I can see them, listen to them, travel to them, pass them, dance around them. I can initiate a rhythm or physical pattern which they can join in. Or I can accent and highlight what they are offering me.

- *If I am creating a solo improvisation on stage, the audience becomes my partner and I can respond to its tempo.*

I see the man in the plaid shirt in the third row. I see the red exit sign and comment either vocally or rhythmically on the woman walking up the aisle to the ladies room.

- *Splitting the attention requires practice.*

As we are noticing and incorporating outside stimuli, we have to keep our inner vessel ready to receive and transform this information, responding with lightning speed to each impression.

- *It's important to tell a story while improvising, to compose extemporaneously a performance with a beginning, middle, and end.*

For instance, the story can be musical with slow, meandering walking steps that use the whole floor. Then, while traveling from stage left to right, develop swing patterns that are strong and syncopated; finally, take center stage in a double time, ending with an exclamation point. Or the story can be literal and narrative, transforming blue moods into blue skies. Perhaps a character who wants to tell a story appears before you. Is it a lost child, a sexy woman, an angry man, or a race horse anxious to hit the track?

- *Create improvised solos.*
- *Trade eight bars with musicians or other dancers.*
- *Listen and share in the spirit of discovery when simultaneously improvising with other dancers.*

Improvisation is really a philosophy of life. An improviser is filled with the intensity of an explorer discovering a new continent or an archaeologist finding a new specimen or a climber looking out over the world with wonder and expanded vision, leaving the smaller self on the ground. But we never leave the tree. The tree is our knowledge and our foundation. So in the meantime:

- *Learn tunes and understand the musical structure of each.*
- *Play tunes with your feet.*
- *Learn Charlie Parker or John Coltrane improvisations with your feet.*
- *Listen to arrangements of Count Basie, Duke Ellington, and Louie Bellson for vamps, grooves, and short licks.*

They use dynamics as a dancer would, with crescendos and diminuendos. The horn section might be playing a riff you can pick up for a background groove. The arrangements might include interesting "hits," "accents," and syncopations. In big band arrangements the solos are shorter and easier to study.

• *Think melodically as well as rhythmically.*

Sing a different tune in your head from what the band is playing. This helps to vary your melodic improvisations and keeps you from playing the same melody over and over.

• *Learn the lyric as well as the melody of a tune.*

The lyric tells the story. Knowing the lyric will help you memorize the tune and give it an emotional context.

• *Sometimes think like a drummer with a full kit, sometimes like a conga drummer, sometimes like a timbale player, a clave player, a saxophone player, a vibes player, or a flute player.*

Each instrument has a different tone and texture as well as different specialties that you can absorb and try to duplicate musically and emotionally.

• *The whole body is your instrument.*

The upper body – the torso, arms, head, and shoulders – can often describe something musically, give accents and express a rhythm figure physically. The expression of the whole body brings an emotional component to the improvisation. A gesture gives a step a personality.

• *Keep practicing three-way listening.*

Listen to yourself through the center of your body, listen to your partner with the left ear, the band with the right ear. Feel the rhythm of your heart trying to speak.

(Refer to instruction videotape *Tap Intensive #3: Improvisation and Afro-Cuban to Bop.*)

COMPOSITION IN TRADITIONAL MODE

The formula for a traditional composition or routine as seen on the vaudeville stage or in variety shows was quite simple and derived from an English, Irish, or Appalachian clogging format in which dancers competed with pre-scribed routines. On the English music hall stages, where many American artists visited, all the numbers were short and succinct. One act after another hardly gave the audi-ence a chance to catch their breath as the performers hit the stage with a bang and left before the applause died down. A dance was called a routine and usually consisted of four eight-bar phrases that were six-bar *time steps* with two-bar *breaks*. Four *time steps* created a thirty-two bar stan-dard chorus. Perhaps the *breaks* would be fancier than the step, perhaps the step would be trickier than the *break*. Maybe each step had a different *break*, or the same *break* might be used after every step.

The BS Chorus and the Old Soft Shoe are very typical of that early formula of one-chorus dances that might open a show or be used in a chorus line. A dance trio might open with a song and perform a one-chorus dance together before each artist did a one-chorus solo. At the end of the act they would join together again for a fast, flashy closer.

The BS Chorus

The BS Chorus as performed by The Copasetics was very fast and used as a *closer, a punctuation,* or *a throwaway* — a good chance for Cookie Cook to throw his hat in the air (and catch it, or not) as an ending. This dance does not need to be a throwaway; it deserves more. If executed at a bright but not breakneck tempo, precisely and with integrity, it is a fabulous chorus.

The *time step* in this dance is performed up on the toes with an elegant carriage, as Bill Robinson would have done it. (He never threw anything away.)

The crossing over of the *cross step* is stylishly exaggerated with the head facing in the opposite direction when closing on the last beat with a snap of the fingers. The *cross step* can be performed with many variations, adding beats within the two-bar phrase. It is an important figure for every dancer to be able to manipulate as a short phrase or to incorporate into an extended phrase that does or does not repeat.

Over the tops is a strenuous step when executed correctly, as in Buster Brown's delivery seen in the documentary *Great Feats of Feet* or in one of Ernie Smith's film clips featuring Raymond Winfield of Tip Tap & Toe. In the most dramatic presentation of *over the tops* the dancer is in a *flat back* position bent over so low that one hand actually brushes the floor as one leg jumps over the other. And one leg does actually jump over the other and doesn't just slide to the side (that's the BS of the BS Chorus).

Trenches or *pulling trenches* get a hand even when executed poorly by a sloppy amateur. Somehow there is a genetic memory in the world of a beautiful *trench,* and the audience is so happy to see any kind of *trench,* anywhere, that they applaud automatically. It's a reflex. But a beautiful *trench* is a joy to behold. A *trench* is pulled with the leg sliding in an arc around to the back. The whole body is suspended on that one leg before the other leg lands and then pulls back immediately for the next transfer. This position too is flat back with the arms swinging in opposition. I have also seen a beautiful variation executed with the arm and leg on the same side pulling in the same direction. The final effect looks like the dancer is skating, and you can hear the "swoosh" as the leg arcs out and slides to the back.

The great wing dancers always hoped the boards were running from upstage to downstage so that when they scraped out on a *wing* or *pulled a trench* the "swoosh" could be heard clearly.

First Eight-bar Step
This one-bar *time step* begins on a pickup: "And a one."
- *shuffle- hop a-flap a-flap step*
  R   L   R   L   R
- *Repeat six times (right and left).*
- *Two-bar break*

The *break* is optional. Sometimes the *time step* just continues, ending on three of the last bar of the eight-bar phrase.

Second Eight-bar Step
The *cross step* also starts on the pickup.
- *heel-shuffle-step brush step shuffle-heel toe-heel step*
  L   R   L   R L R   L
- *Repeats — right, left, right*
- *Two-bar break*

The *break* is made up of two of the first *time steps* or a variation.

Third Eight-bar Step
The *wing step* also begins on a pickup.
- *hop shuffle-step brush-wing brush-step*
  L   R   L R   L

- *shuffle-step shuffle-step*
    R   L
- *Repeat three times.*
- *Two-bar break*

    The *break* is the same as the last two steps.

    Fourth Eight-bar Step

The fourth step is divided into three parts:

    I. Two bars in half time

- *One over the top — begin on one.*
- *jump-step slide-back jump over*
    R   L   R
- *jump-step slide-back jump over*
    L   R   L
- *strike-toe jump step slide back jump over*
    R   L   R   L   R
- *jump slide back step*
    L   R   L

    2. One bar in half time

- *Pull four trenches.*

    3. One-bar in half time

- *Shave-and-a-hair-cut break*
- *Both feet jump into pull-up cramp roll with heels.*
- *brush heel step*
    R   L R

The Old Soft Shoe

As Honi Coles would tell it, the Old Soft Shoe is a dance of grace, beauty, and motion. Originally it was indeed a *soft shoe*, performed in shoes without taps. As is the case with the BS Chorus, many of the figures are part of the tap dance vernacular and can be performed in a classic routine or incorporated into contemporary compositions. In the classic Soft Shoe that Honi and I performed in our concert, as well as our more contemporary version to "Taking a Chance on Love" that followed, the *soft shoe breaks* often use traveling running steps to close a figure rather than hard fast punctuation.

I love to perform the Old Soft Shoe to "In A Sentimental Mood" or a slow version of "Tea for Two" after singing the poignant verse. This Copasetic version of the old *soft shoe*, though often performed as a parody to "Way Down Upon the Sewanee River," is another classic one-chorus routine of the vaudeville era. It deserves to be performed with virtuosity and respect.

Louie Simms was the most unusual *soft shoe* dancer I ever saw. He not only danced the *soft shoe* without taps on his shoes, he executed the rhythms in the air with his legs describing the rhythm but not sounding it out. He also performed this *soft shoe* bent over so low to the ground that we often thought he would fall over. I love to fall way over on the entrance to the *break*, lifting my body up into a great sweep for the triplets at the end. The rhythms of a *soft shoe* have a lilt because of the frequent use of triplets. Traveling in triplets gives the dance its grace and fluidity.

First Eight-bar Step
This two-bar *soft shoe time step* begins on a pickup, "a four and a one."
- *brush-back-step   brush-over-step   step*
       R   L   R
- *brush-back-step   brush-over-step   step*
       L   R   L

- *brush–back–step   brush–over–step   step*
     R   L   R
- *brush–back–step   step   brush–over–step   step*
     L   R   L   R
- *Repeat three times RLR.*
- *Two-bar break*
  Paddle turn to the right and left: begins on a pick-up, "a one."
- *brush–step   brush–step–step   brush–step–step   brush–step–step*
     R   L   R   L   R   L   R

Second Eight-bar Step

This step begins on a pickup, "a one."
- *brush–back heel   brush–side–heel   brush–front–heel   slap out,*
     R   L   R   L   R   L   R
- *brush–back–step   brush–back–step   shuffle–hop–cross   step*
     L   R   L R L   R
- *brush–step   brush–step   step   shuffle hop shuffle–step brush*
     L   R   L   R L R   L
- *hop (turn) step step step ball-change.*
     R   L R L R L

Repeat this to the left.

Third Eight-bar Step

A *scissors step* in a cutting motion begins on a pickup, "a one."
- *brush–step–back (with feet turned out)*
     R
- *step   step (with feet turned in, in a cutting motion)*
     L   R

Repeat four times RLRL.

A Honi Coles variation follows, in double time. Repeat three times RLR:

- *dig–brush–heel–toe slap*
  R   L R R
- *On the last execution add a* flap-ball-change
                               L   R   L

Repeat the *scissors* three times then end with

- *brush–step   step*
      L   R
- *Two-bar break*
- *brush step   brush step-step   shuffle hop   shuffle-step brush*
      L   R L   R L   R L
- *hop walk walk walk . . . (in a circle)*
    R   L   R   L

Fourth Eight-bar Step

The step begins on a pickup, "a four and a one."

- *shuffle-ball-heel step kickback-slap foot step kickback-slap*
         R   L   R   R   L
- *step   clap clap (over and under the knee)   step*
    L   R   R
- *brush step   brush step step shuffle hop shuffle step   brush*
       L   R R L   R   L   R   L
- *hop step-turn step step*
     R L R L

Repeat on right side.

- *Two-bar break*

The next step begins on a pickup, "a one."

- *brush step   brush step   step   shuffle hop*
       L   R   L   R L
- *shuffle-step   shuffle-step*
      R   L

- *running steps in a triplet rhythm*
     LRL RLR LRL R

The *soft shoe breaks* often use traveling running steps to close
a figure rather than hard fast punctuation

   (Refer to instruction tape *Tap Intensive 2* plus *Great Feats of
Feet: Portrait of the Jazz Tap Dancer, Featuring Honi Coles and The
Copasetics.*)

THE WALK AROUND OR THE COLES STROLL

I was very fortunate to have the opportunity of performing
duet concerts with Honi Coles from 1978 until he was
crippled by a stroke in 1987. It certainly made me a perfectionist trying to live up to his standards. By the end of his
performing career he had eliminated all but the essentials
of what he wanted to convey. Often he approached a dance
with such elegant simplicity that the audience felt they
were right there onstage performing the steps with him,
until of course he flashed into one of his faster-than-the-
speed-of-light figures.

   The Coles Stroll is a simple, elegant, perfect composition that Honi created for actors and singers to dance on
The Perry Como Show. By adding another beat and syncopation every eight bars, these beginners learned to dance by
the time they got to the end of the routine. The Copasetics
opened their shows with this dance, as did Honi and I
when we performed our duet concerts *Singin' Swingin' &
Wingin'* and *Sounds In Motion.*

   When Cookie Cook, Bubba Gaines, and Honi Coles
performed and taught workshops for the official opening

of The Dancing Theatre in the spring of 1974, Cookie taught this dance to a group of my beginner students, half of them dressed in straw hats and sandals, cut-off jeans, and sneakers. Only a few wore tap shoes. Cookie always taught class with his hat in his hand, periodically placing it on top of his head, tossing it on top of his head, or tossing it in the air and letting it fall. He had a proprietary attitude about the Walk Around. I didn't realize then that this was Honi's creation because Cookie told me it was a gift from him and that I could teach it in all my classes. As The Copasetics became more in demand for concerts and performed this dance regularly, Honi finally put his claim on it and renamed it the Coles Stroll.

When performing on tour with The Copasetics, we opened our show entering from stage right, walking into a circle. Usually the lineup was Honi, Cookie, Bubba, Buster, and me. Being white, female, and blonde I was a shock to the audience and always got a laugh on my entrance. Women had not yet gained credibility, and in the public's perception all tappers were male, black, and usually old. At least this opening number gave people a chance to get used to me before I performed my solo.

The Coles Stroll is a dance of introduction — a circle dance in which each dancer can be introduced with a little aside every time he or she turns the corner to face the audience. It is a dance that comments on itself, that instructs the viewer on how tap dancers use their feet, from the simplest to the most complicated manipulations. The composition builds around the simple walk and adds a beat every eight bars. After a chorus and a half of "A Train" the dancers come down stage, traveling nonchalantly into a straight line for the elegant razzle-dazzle of the last sixteen bars.

Charles Cook and Ernest Brown teaching jazz dancing at The Dancing Theatre during the shoot for the documentary "Great Feats of Feet." At far left of students is Dorothy Wasserman, at far right Jane Goldberg.

The Coles Stroll has been taught to dancers all over the world. We still use it as an opening number for many of our festival shows. Most of the acts on any bill know the Coles Stroll, and we enjoy opening our concerts with a tribute to one of our great tap masters.

I must offer a disclaimer as I begin to break down this dance. Honi never used words like *shuffle, hop,* or *ball change.* He would become insulted if you tried to force him to express himself in tap nomenclature or even ask where the *one* was in a phrase. He only described his steps by scatting them and insisted that you must simply feel the step, and this was the way he taught me when I was a young girl. I hope he will forgive me for giving so much description to this dance, but if he were here, we would have a little argument, and I would insist that it's hard to feel a dance on paper.)

I. With his artful intelligence Honi started the dance with a simple walk for eight bars. As they walked, the dancers interjected their personalities, relaxed, and moved with personal style.

2. Next he introduced a *heel toe* on each foot (much simpler to execute than a *toe heel*).

 Sheee bup Sheee bup

3. The third eight-bar step includes more beats and is the first syncopated rhythm:

• *heel-toe brush-heel heel-toe*

 Sheee bup Shube do Bop

4. The fourth eight-bar step brings the syncopation to both feet:

• *brush-heel heel-toe brush-heel heel toe*

 Shube do Bop Shube do Bop

Bubba Gaines usually spoke to the audience as he turned the corner on this step: "So easy when you know how."

 Shube do Bop Shube do Bop

5. The rhythm doesn't change and nothing is added, but the heel becomes a hop:

• *brush hop heel-toe brush hop heel-toe*

 Shube do Bop Shube do Bop

Just as he was about to make the turn Honi would shout out, "Now we're getting energetic."

6. The next six bars are a challenge:

- *brush-hop-heel-toe toe jump heel-toe*
  Shubadobop Sha padobop   Subadobop Sha padobop

Somebody would say, "Now we're getting fancy." The final two bars of the phrase brings everyone into a straight line with a return to:

- *brush-hop heel-toe brush-hop heel-toe*
  Shuba do Bop Shuba do Bop

7. For the next eight bars we organize into a straight line. We get subtle and dainty as we brush the heel into a tiptoe from side to side across the stage.

- *Toe-heel   toe-heel   toe-heel   toe-heel*
  Dee ba   Dee ba   Dee ba   Dee ba

The hands and the head are placed to the right when traveling to the left, and to the left when traveling to the right.

  Deeba Deeba Deeba Deeba

8. For the last eight-bar step the dancers introduce the audience to an articulated phrase of three steps beginning on the right foot, left and right:

- *shuffle-ball-heel-punch shuffle-ball-heel-punch shuffle-ball-heal toe-heel*
      R   L   L   R   R   R
- *toe-heel toe-heel step*
      L   R   L

  Shado badebop Shado badebop Shado bade do bade do bade dop

  The final two-bar break finishes emphatically.

- *shuffle-ball-heel step brush-heel brush-step brush-heel brush-step (cross)*
        R   L R L R   L R L

  (cross) shuffle-ball-heel toe step.
        R   L L

  Shadobade bop breeup de-dop breeup de-dop Shadobade dop schlop

This two-chorus dance is a classic. Its theme is clear. It is a walking dance. As Honi liked to say at the end of the

dance, "If you can walk you can dance – proof positive."
Just as the Coles Stroll was and still is a great opener, in
fifty years we have never found a better closer than the
Shim Sham. Though the Shim Sham knows many variations and claims many composers, Leonard Reed created
one of the first versions. Honi always created variations and
exit steps, like the *Suzi Q*, with the dancers waving and saying, "Bye bye." At the climax the dancers take three steps
backward, face the audience and bow. These little grace
notes of variations give the clue to who put this particular
show together.

The Dance In Tap Dance

From the Vernacular to the Conceptual

Yes, we do say tap *dance*. We don't only compose rhythms
and execute them, we dance them, express them throughout
the body from the legs, the pelvis, the hips, the torso, the
shoulders, the limbs and the head.

I find it essential to link the style of the movement to
the style and period of the music and rhythms. If I am
working in a swing vein, I will incorporate the vernacular
dance of that period into the rhythms; in fact they might
initiate the rhythms. The Charleston, the Lindy, and the
Big Apple were danced in the ballrooms and living rooms
in the 1920s through the 1940s. At the same time, tap was
developing its sophistication and musicality. Many tap
dancers, including Honi Coles, first danced the Charleston
on street corners and at house parties, eventually putting

taps into the Charleston to give it more power and also give an edge to their competitions at amateur shows.

Cookie Cook and Brownie Brown added only a little footwork to their vernacular jazz dance Old Man Time, or "Oo bee da." The Shim Sham Shimmy and the Old Soft Shoe can be danced as vernacular jazz dances, with or without taps.

The tack Annie, the second step in the Shim Sham, brings the foot to the back while the chest pushes forward. This version comes with a lot of stories attached. Cookie says that the move was inspired by Annie, a big fat woman who lived in Chicago. She was often in trouble with the law, and when the police arrived at her door she would attack, butting them with her big sumptuous tummy – hence, the attack of the *tack Annie.* Some dancers put a shaking *shimmy* to the shoulders on the *tack Annie,* some insist the right move is *pull it,* a gesture that pulls the arm back to the hip with the foot. Just to confuse people, I execute a separate version for each two-bar repetition.

At the end of the tap Shim Sham, The Copasetics would often put a swing chorus with a *boogie back, boogie front,* and end with *shorty George* and a *Suzie Q* exit.

When I choreographed and performed the minuet in *The Morton Gould Tap Concerto,* the physical expression that initiated the rhythms was ballet. In my "6 Against 2 Mambo" composition for the American Tap Dance Orchestra, I composed the melody around Afro-Cuban rhythms and mambo moves then initiated the footwork.

Many tap dancers came from the modern dance tradition. For instance, Lynn Dally's tap compositions are distinguished by long sweeping gestures and carefully conceived and staged choreography. Sam Webbers' delivery is upright and balletic. Dancing on the balls of his feet, he executes *shuffles* so dense they are heard as arpeggios. He travels so deftly and swiftly across the stage one might think he had attached his taps to toe shoes. Linda Sohl Donnell often uses exotic music and movement to distinguish the country of rhythmic origin that inspires her compositional choreographies.

In my dance the "Flying Turtles," the physical expression came first. Inspired by my early saturation in West African movements and pantomime, I found that these shapes and rhythms helped me to build a narrative that was not presentational but was internal, eternal, and spiritual.

Gregory Hines and Savion Glover found physical forms — the *dance* in tap dance — in contemporary vernacular movement and contemporary music. Savion, with his dreadlocks and funk street moves, connects tap dance once again to the popular music of its time. With a bare chest and head covered in a bandanna, Max Pollak will often open his presentations with hard-edged ritualistic Afro-Cuban moves.

Whatever the physical expression, it gives power to the taps only if there is something essential, honest, or conceptually imperative to the forms. Giving shape to the arms and torso just because you have to do something with them, or have to put them someplace, is not enough.

(Refer to the video instruction and concert tapes *Tap Intensive #1* ["Vernacular Dance and Time Steps"], *Two Takes on Tap, American Landscape, Cantata & the Blues, Great Feats of Feet.*)

HESITATION & ANTICIPATION

There is a moment when our talent runs out, when we have used all the resources that nature, our ancestors, our genes, and our intuition have made available to us, and nothing new appears.

• *This is the moment the real work begins. Using the mind as well as the body finally becomes a necessity.*

One of my biggest challenges came with an insight I was given during a tour in London of *Sounds in Motion* in duet with Honi Coles. As we performed, many opportunities for collaborations and improvisations presented themselves. Sometimes the musicians played our music so poorly we would have to improvise half of our show. After a few weeks on tour, performing every night, I was beginning to hear myself. I heard the same patterns recurring over and over. It also seemed that my phrases weren't succinct; I was stamping too much. I could hear the frustration in my feet; something was missing; I was stuck again.

With some reservation I asked Honi if he had any suggestions. He seldom commented on my dancing. He never told me whether I did great or was really awful. He expected me to be my own teacher. But I was desperate, so I pushed him into giving me some help. "Is it my imagination or is there something very wrong with the execution of my improvisations?"

He said, "I don't know what you're talking about; you danced your can off." After a short pause he continued, "But I think your style is too crowded." I was shocked, because he was the master of crowding every beat. He said,

"Yes I know, you got it from me, but it's not a good idea to crowd so much."

This was, indeed, a conundrum – a statement to ponder – as I knew he would never explain himself or elaborate. I had to find out for myself if I was indeed crowding too much and what exactly that meant. And if I was crowding, what should I do about it? Finally, after audio taping my rehearsals and listening rather than watching myself on videotape, I began to hear what Honi was talking about: what the difference was between his crowding and my crowding, why his approach sounded so much better than mine.

I saw that he took a breath before entering from single time to double time. There was a moment of hesitation, an inward breath, before an explosion of speed. Once again I returned to my favorite jazz discs and listened to how Dizzy did it, how Count Basie and Oscar Peterson broke down the time and doubled the time. Ahhhhh ... it was with hesitation and anticipation. I found that hesitation and anticipation were as important to making a performance swing as were the accents or how many syncopated, offbeat phrases you invented. Just as in the blues: all good blues singers leave space between their phrases. The phrases appear in a spontaneous rush rather than a carefully planned placement on the right note.

For months I improvised to the blues, sang the blues, and composed rhythms to the blues. Finally, I went back to my earlier material and adjusted the way I went into a phrase and came out of it. Suddenly everything came into focus and my compositions didn't appear crowded anymore. My improvisations were more deliberate, less frantic.

Little devices, like leaving a space instead of executing the last quarter note before going into double time, made the double time much faster, more punctuated. I waited, waited, and waited. And then rushed. Hesitation and anticipation — how much clearer everything sounded after a year of working on this.

• *Leave space. Take a breath and then rush in.*

CREATING AN ENSEMBLE:
THE EQUILIBRATION OF VIBRATIONS

• *"Equilibrate the vibrations" is an expression that I like to use when dealing with disparate group energies.*

One dancer might have very subtle movements, another very broad and brazen. One dancer might have bounce in his style, another a glide. For the purposes of ensemble work I ask them to blend their energies, the subtle dancer to expand, the brazen hoofer to contain, just a little. The objective of great tone, texture, and expression lies in an entire ensemble's ability to harmonize, to equilibrate — to achieve equilibrium.

• *An ensemble needs to practice together regularly.*

As in a modern dance company, a tap dance company needs to take class together with the same teacher/choreographer so that everyone agrees on the same methods of articulation. A consistent core group assures the development of that second nature that enables dancers to anticipate the shifts and changes of the dancers next to them.

Though I often held auditions, I rarely took dancers who had not studied with me or someone of the same tradition, i.e., Leon Collins, Honi Coles, Cookie Cook, or Eddie

Brown. Those who turned out for auditions just to get this gig before they went to the next gig were almost always recognizable and were rarely accepted into our company.

* *When I create choreography for my company or am commissioned to set a piece on another company, we all participate in the tap warm-up.*
* *For our rehearsals and performances I insist that everyone wear the same type of shoe and that their taps be tightened to the same degree. This affects the tone and the pitches.*

I, of course, prefer the flat oxford shoe, and my favorite tap at the moment is the Rayow Tele Tone Tap with one screw (it must be put on very carefully). I have designed the shoes my dancers wear. The "Brenda Bufalino" tap shoe is presently manufactured by Leo's Dancewear.

* *When the ensemble dances in unison I want five, nine, or forty-five dancers to sound like one, with everyone hitting the same pitch in their shuffle high notes and bass low notes. That's why we all wear the same shoe and why I developed the Shuffle Scale.*

Especially for my compositions that include counterpoint, the pitch and timbre of the tap is vitally important, as is how hard or soft the attack on the floor.

* *An ensemble of dancers can give energy to each other. The group swells like a great wave that delicately separates when it reaches the shore.*

Costuming for a tap dance requires a great deal of thought. If the dance is a narrative, perhaps a couple dance from the swing era that wishes to evoke romance budding at a party, this calls for very specific costuming. In Deborah Mitchell's beautiful "Moon Suite," for the New Jersey Tap Ensemble, the women wear ball gowns, and the men white dinner jackets and black pants. For my swing dances that are simply about the rhythms and movements of the period, the dancers all wear the same costume.

Except for my tap opera, which is a mythical work, I have kept the conceit of an orchestra, and we, of course, dance in tails: white tails, gray tails, or black tails. We vary our costume with formal white vests or checkered vests or turtleneck shirts — but always tails. The tails signify two things at once: birds in flight for my creature pieces and very elegant musicians entering the symphonic stage with their violins. As costuming reflects the taste of the choreographer and the needs of the dance my suggestions are quite simple.

- *The costume should never upstage the dance.*
- *The denser the rhythm, the simpler the costume.*

I do not have any standard for body type or height, weight, hair color, race, or gender. The simplicity of our costume gives the company enough of a uniform look for my taste. With the work in equilibrating the vibrations, it is my hope that each ensemble dancer will not have to give up his or her individual style, only blend with the rest for the work at hand.

- *When the dancers in the Orchestra began to create and perform their own solos I was overjoyed to see that each dancer had maintained his or her own character and personality as well as particular rhythmic and performance values.*

This is, perhaps, what I consider my greatest achievement as a teacher and choreographer. They don't look like me. If they did I'd probably stop dancing.

CHOREOGRAPHY AND COMPOSITION:
VOICE AND CHOICE

I like each composition to have its own uniqueness and character, lending variety and different emotional qualities to an evening's performance.

• *Counterpoint has always been my signature. A successful counterpoint composition is highly complex because you are making the many into one.*

• *There is no margin for error in a counterpoint. Placing rhythms against each other in this way clears up any ambiguity about a syncopation or the value of an eighth note and its placement in the phrase.*

The audience knows an especially successful counterpoint when they hear it. If many rhythms building to a crescendo blend together as one, with a dynamic and viscerally penetrating energy, there is always applause. If there is no blend and the rhythms do not lay over each other perfectly, the audience is confused and their minds travel to the refreshment counter.

To get to the next step of our personal evolution there is always some discomfort. We do not necessarily evolve in an orderly or predictable way, and neither should a rhythm, theme, or narrative.

• *I do not want to know what will happen, I want to find out what happened.*

After arriving at a concept, I create and teach a new work with a flurry. I've always been very lucky that way. The composition just appears in my feet: my body follows, and then my mind follows. I have never planned a class or a rehearsal. True to my character, I am an improviser.

Working in this way is sometimes tough on my dancers. The work comes out fast and rough, and, until I am finished with a piece, I don't want to work on finesse or detail. For ten years I was very fortune to have Barbara Duffy as a dance captain. After I created the patterns on the dancers, she polished them down to the last detail. Often they were so polished I'd have to rough them up again. And she'd have to polish them up again. That was the beautiful way in which we worked.

• *It is said that form follows function. In most of my tap dances the body follows the feet and not the other way around. If the body is relaxed it will find its form from the exaggeration of the weight shift.*

Sometimes in rehearsal I would sit quietly and watch the dancers moving through their patterns. When I saw some physical expression that I really liked on a particular dancer, I would ask the other dancers to experiment and find that in their own bodies. I have always felt that, although the rhythms must be completely finite and exact, how a dancer moves should be individual. The dancers are only asked to equilibrate the vibrations.

Some of the most serene moments of my life have been playing the drums on stage for the Orchestra. I will always feel immensely gratful to the dancers for being the palette for my paintings, the symphony for my compositions.

Collaborating on Text, Music, and Choreography for "Clara's Dream ... A Jazz Tap Nutcracker"

In 1999, tap dancer and festival producer Drika Overton of Portsmouth, New Hampshire, was ready to actualize her dream of creating a tap *Nutcracker* in collaboration with five other choreographers: Dean Diggens, Jeannie Hill, Josh

Hilberman, Bob E. Thomas, and me. Original music and arrangements, based on Duke Ellington's jazz version of the *Nutcracker*, would be created by Paul Arslanian. I thought this sounded like an exciting project, homegrown and organic, so I agreed to participate in this complicated and time-consuming collaborative experiment.

We six artists sequestered ourselves in a cottage by the sea for a week to write a libretto and conceive the concepts for the dances and the music. Somehow, by mixing and matching our disparate energies and expertise on each piece, we created a harmonious successful theatrical production, which has been performed on tour for four Christmas seasons. Jeannie, after the birth of her little girl, had to relinquish her starring role of Clara to Katy Yoder, a young and charming ingénue, who also costumed our show of twelve dancers and eight musicians. In 2001, naming ourselves "The Mad Theatricals," this collaborative created the scenario for a vaudeville show during a weeklong retreat at the Yoder farm in Maine. *The Music Hall Follies: A Vaudeville in 9 Acts* was presented at the Portsmouth Percussive Dance Festival in 2002. Our production in-cluded a chorus, and special guest artists.

This collaboration has not been without its trials and tribulations, arguments and reconciliation's. All of our temperaments and talents are extreme, but we have agreed that each of us should express ourselves without reservation in the creation of each piece. We then shape and whittle down the hard edges so each piece fits together, a true equilibration of vibrations, both of personalities and talents.

(Refer to American Tap Dance Orchestra's concert videotapes *ATDO in Performance, American Landscape, Two Takes on Tap, Someone Stole the Baby.*)

The Music Of Tap Dance

We tap dancers call ourselves musicians because we play rhythms with our feet. But what does it mean to be a musician? What are the responsibilities of musicianship? What do musicians know that tap dancers should know?

- *Jazz musicians have memorized a library full of standards (songs in a standard format of thirty-two bars, or twelve- bar blues).*

The tap dancer should own two or three songbooks, learn hundreds of songs, and listen to vocalists to learn the lyrics to those songs and study phrasing. It is important to know standards that musicians are familiar with in case there is no time for rehearsal or you are improvising at a tap jam. It is also important to know which standards best represent the groove or pocket you like to dance in. Singing the lyric of a tune silently while dancing helps to create a tap story.

- *Musicians know how to read and write music.*

It is important for the tap dancer to know how to read enough to locate each eight-bar phrase in the tune. The better you can read, the better the communication between you and the musician.

- *Musicians enjoy playing with each other and understand the nature of the rhythm section, (piano, bass and drums.)*

I love improvising simultaneously with other dancers. Trading bars is fun but it is often competitive. Simultaneous improvisation is very free, but it requires listening and communicating, not always soloing but blending with the other dancers' many rhythms to create a dynamic musical symmetry.

• *Musicians understand how to work together, how to support each other and give each other space.*

I like dancing with one instrument at a time, leaving space as in a conversation, or sometimes responding to a pattern I have just heard. It is easier for a musician to listen to me when just the two of us perform together.

• *Musicians elaborate on, or participate in, a soloist's improvisation by comping or accompanying.*

When the pianist is taking a two-chorus solo, the drummer and bass player listen intently. The right boost and support helps the soloist relax and feel at home with the harmonies and structure of a tune, so he can be free with his creativity. If it is the bass player's turn to solo, the pianist and drummer appreciate the delicate tone of the contrabass and play softly in the background so the bassist can hear himself and build confidently on a theme. Musicians expect as much from dancers. The dancer is a member of the ensemble, playing his or her instrument out in front only because more space is needed.

So what should tap dancers do when they get up to perform their set dances or to improvise freely with the band?

• *Call a tune and set the time.*

The best way to set the time in 4/4 is to call out single time and double time — I 2 I234. I do not ask the band-leader to remember the time we set in rehearsal. I might want to change it slightly when it comes time for my performance, or the band might have just played very fast for the last act and can't adjust to my tempo unless I set it firmly. I always feel the necessity to set the time and the responsibility of dancing to the time I have set.

• *If you have set the time too fast, do not ask the band to slow down.*

The band is comprised of separate musicians, who can't all slow down or speed up at the same time in the same way. It's almost impossible to get into a groove if you try to change the tempo in the middle of a tune. Learn how to call it out clearly and then deal with whatever one you have set. The dancer sets the tempo and, right or wrong, dances the result.

In my performance, if the tempo is too slow or too fast to dance my dance, I either improvise a new dance to suit the tempo or stop and start again. Perhaps I might dance a chorus to the tempo everyone is playing and then signal the band to "lay out." I can then dance a cappella for a while and reset the tempo. The aim is to do this seamlessly, so that I will still appear in control, and the audience or the band members do not feel uncomfortable.

- *Once you have called a tune, dance phrases that relate to the melody and harmonies as well as the time feel.*
- *Listen and respond to what each musician is playing.*

The dancer does not just dance on and on, louder and louder, using the band as a drum machine that is keeping the pulse. The band is not your metronome.

- *If you want a complicated arrangement, hire an instrumentalist before the gig, lay out what you want, ask for suggestions, and have him or her write out the arrangement for you.*

It is unreasonable to ask the band to create a complicated arrangement for you on the spot.

- *If you have an arrangement, or even just a lead sheet with the melody and format written out, you should be able to explain your music to the band leader and, if necessary, to the other band members.*

For instance, if the structure is three choruses, explain what is happening in each chorus: first chorus melody, second chorus stop time, third chorus melody. If the band is not given any instructions they will play the melody, which is often called the head, and then improvise the rest of the choruses around the melody.

• *Words like* pianissimo *or* fortissimo *can be put into your arrangement.*

If you have a series of complicated figures, you might like the band to play pianissimo (softly). If you would like to have a big dramatic ending for the last eight bars of every chorus, your arrangement there would say fortissimo (very loud). Remember, not making musical choices is a choice. If you want to dance full out for unlimited choruses, with everyone just blowing, you have made a choice to just let things happen as they will. Don't complain when you come off stage that you didn't like what the band played.

I suggest to students that they learn a second instrument. I practice my reading skills, create arrangements, and write original music on the piano or my concertina. Once you begin to really play with musicians it's not about steps anymore; it's about phrasing and developing the melody, dancing on musical structures, and listening to each of the other instruments and to yourself.

When rehearsing with the musicians it is first important to know who the leader of the group is. I've made some very bad mistakes talking to each musician without talking to the leader first. If it's the pianist in a rhythm section, this makes the job fairly easy; if the leader is a bass player or a drummer, it is more difficult to discuss your arrangements. Nevertheless, it must be done this way.

Darrell Grant was the first pianist who fully aligned himself with my company. He was young and fresh from college. We learned from each other. His enthusiastic temperament gave me the freedom to experiment and to ask his advice when I got stuck on a musical choice, like a particular vamp in 2/4 that he could identify easier than I, even though I created it. He would get so excited during a performance he might scream out, "I love this stuff." Darrell was with us for three years and helped me write and create arrangements for *The American Landscape.*

After our Joyce performances, Darrell moved to Oregon. We were desperate to find a new pianist for our touring season. Because our band consisted only of piano and bass, our pianist needed to be a soloist and had to play with the fullness of a whole orchestra at times. Barbara Duffy, the company's dance captain, convinced Frank Kimbrough to join us because he was just such a pianist. He had been playing solo piano at the Corner Bar on Bleeker and LaGuardia in New York City for quite a few years and was mentoring with the great blind pianist Lance Hayward. We felt fortunate that Frank agreed to join us because he also brought improvisational skills and versatility.

When we began rehearsal, Frank seemed rather surly to me, a little arrogant. He tried to read the charts that Darrell had left behind, but the scratchy charts and clatter of the taps frustrated him. I started singing the arrangement and said, "Right here it goes 'Shoobab dee dow.'" He looked down at his still fingers and replied, "'Shoo bap dee dow' don't mean shit to me." I was just about to show him the door when I looked at Barbara's pained expression and unspoken plea, "Please be nice ... pulease work it out." I calmed down and tried to describe our arrangement in musical language instead of rhythmically scatting. Frank Kimbrough played brilliantly with us for the next eight years. This first encounter became an inside joke, illustrating the typical friction between dancer and musician. We dancers are often defensive about what we don't know, not realizing that musicians have their own insecurities. Dancers can facilitate the communication process by learning the musicians' language.

I really learned to appreciate the difficulties musicians have in playing with, or collaborating with, tap dancers when I accompanied the ATDO on the drums for an entire season. I had often wondered why musicians didn't understand where my "one" was in the music or didn't seem to be listening to my rhythms. I discovered it is not always possible to hear where the dancer is. I also discovered how important it is for the dancers' rhythms to be clear. An occasional look or gesture to the band often helps to communicate the rhythms or where I want them to play soft or loud, or "lay out." We can talk to them as we dance, with our gestures as well as our feet. We must learn how to conduct while we are performing and stay in contact with the band while we are reaching out to the audience, which is *no small feat.*

A wonderful performance is the result of a successful collaboration. When I leave the stage and feel as if my performance were effortless, it is usually because the musicians were so skillful and we have succeeded in locking in a groove; we have interpreted the tune in a mutually sympathetic way because we have listened to each other. When it is right, I am filled with gratitude and think I could dance forever. I never forget to say thank you.

~

Summation

IT'S AMAZING, WHEN SOMEONE ASKS ME how long I've been tap dancing, that the answer is … sixty years. Every day of at least twenty-five of those years I have asked myself if I think I should continue. When I am tired I say, "I'm too tired to dance," as I'm tying up my shoes. When I get a stupid, uninformed review I say, "I'll show them, I'll never dance again," as I'm tying up my shoes. When I have run out of ideas and seem to be in a rut and say, "What's the use I'm all used up, I'll never dance again," I find myself tying up my shoes.

And they are everywhere, these oh-so-solid oxford shoes. They are under my bed, under my couch, under my kitchen table, in the trunk of my car, and in all of my closets. I hardly ever get rid of an old pair of tap shoes; their memories are sacred.

Sometimes it seems such a foolish thing for a mature adult to do. Funny really … this tapping sound from the feet created by lifting the leg and prancing, controlled by fast or slow changes of weight. Tapping while dancing, tapping out a rhythm, tapping out many rhythms — simply that, tapping out rhythms with the feet while shifting weight rhythmically. Feeling the rhythm connect to the

237

heartbeat, like the tapping of a branch on my front door. Tapping sounds like rain on the windowpane, sometimes blending with the sound of a brook, the rushing or dripping of a faucet. Tapping connected to a greater force, blending with other forces. A fugue of rhythms, building on each other, building to a crescendo ... descending to a diminuendo. Tapping into the source, tapping with force into the beginnings, tapping with a whisper at the closing.